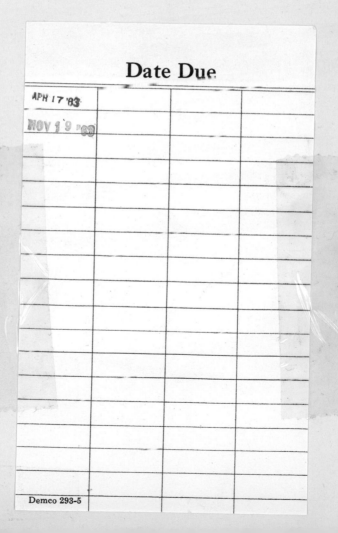

Date Due

AMERICA'S RULE
IN THE
WORLD ECONOMY

BOOKS BY ALVIN H. HANSEN

FULL RECOVERY OR STAGNATION?
FISCAL POLICY AND BUSINESS CYCLES
AMERICA'S ROLE IN THE WORLD ECONOMY

with HARVEY S. PERLOFF

STATE AND LOCAL FINANCE IN THE
NATIONAL ECONOMY

AMERICA'S ROLE
IN THE
WORLD ECONOMY

By ALVIN H. HANSEN

Littauer Professor of Political Economy, Harvard University
and
Special Economic Adviser, Board of Governors
of the Federal Reserve System

NEW YORK

W · W · NORTON & COMPANY · INC ·

Contents

THERE can be little question that we are currently passing through one of the most critical periods, if indeed not the most critical period, of modern times. Looking back over the events of the last few years it may be seriously questioned whether as a people we have any real understanding of how dreadfully near we came, not once but several times, to the brink of disaster. Suppose the robot planes had been developed a few years earlier and had been thrown into the aerial attack on Britain in the summer and autumn of 1940; suppose we had not succeeded through accurate aerial bombardment in reducing the robot menace, when it did come, to perhaps 10 per cent of the dimensions that had been planned by the Nazis; suppose the British leaders had in the hour of crisis in 1940 not decided to stand firm; suppose Hitler had not made the mistake of attacking Russia in 1941; and finally, suppose that we had yielded as a people, as could well have been the case, to the powerful voices of dissension, inaction and isolation in our own midst. Looking back over it all and considering the whole course of events, we can indeed be thankful that we have escaped. But it is incredible as we look back over it all that the Allies who fought World War I to a successful conclusion should have allowed themselves to drift along until we came perilously near to utter disaster.

I cannot help believing that this terrific experience has sunk deep into the consciousness of the people of the United

States and indeed of the peoples of the United Nations. Two world wars within a single generation could not fail to make an indelible impression and to convince even the most naïve and careless optimist that it is no easy task to maintain the peace of the world and that to accomplish this task it is absolutely essential to enter into close collaboration and continuous co-operation with other countries.

Such international co-operation involves, everyone is agreed, a world political organization designed to insure, by the application of force when necessary, the peace of the world. It is not, however, so well understood that the permanence and workability of a world security organization must be reinforced and sustained by a world economic program. Unless we can solve our economic problems we shall not succeed in maintaining the peace of the world merely by setting up, no matter how well designed, a world political organization.

I have called this book *America's Role in the World Economy*. This title underscores the fact that world prosperity and world stability depend in no small measure upon (*a*) the achievement of full employment within the United States, and (*b*) the active and wholehearted co-operation of the United States in the formation and development of international economic organizations designed to insure the workability of a new world order.

This book is addressed to the general intelligent reader. It is not a book for the specialist. It is intended to help that ever growing and ever more influential group of people who, despite a good educational background, find a great difficulty in making their way through the intricacies of economic discussions. Everywhere people are more and more eager to acquire a background of knowledge and competence in economic matters sufficient to enable them to judge for themselves the merits of conflicting and opposing arguments. I have advanced in these pages a positive thesis of my own, but I hope that in so doing I have aided readers who do not follow me in all my conclusions to think through the problems for themselves. It is not a difficult book, and I hope that it may dispel in some measure the belief that economic problems are so complex that they cannot be understood by the general reader.

It is imperative that we *do* in the generation that lies ahead of us greatly increase the general knowledge and understanding of our citizens in these matters; for unless we do so, we shall not succeed in achieving the great goals of full employment, rising living standards and economic stability in a free democratic society. Freedom and democracy cannot be achieved, as some would have us believe, by going back to laissez faire and noninterventionist policies In the modern world, freedom and democracy can survive only by a positive program of action firmly based on the broad education and understanding of the masses of our people and on their active and self-disciplined participation in the formation of public policy.

In my thinking about these problems I have had many discussions with innumerable friends from all over the world. I am especially indebted, however, to my own colleagues in Harvard University and in the Federal Reserve System. I wish especially to express my appreciation to Miss Phyllis Bramlet and to Miss Jane Hutchins for efficient help in preparing the manuscript for the press and for making the index. Finally, I must acknowledge the invaluable facilities placed at my disposal both by the Graduate School of Public Administration of Harvard University and by the Board of Governors of the Federal Reserve System.

Alvin H. Hansen

PART ONE

POSTWAR HOPES AND FEARS

CHAPTER I

THE OUTLOOK FOR ECONOMIC SECURITY AND WORLD PEACE

INTERNATIONAL security and world peace cannot be achieved except through international co-operation. This is obvious, but we shall need to reiterate it again and again in the generation that lies ahead.

It is of the utmost importance continually to keep before us the fact that the maintenance of peace is no easy matter. We were naïve after World War I. We thought we had fought a war to end all war. As a nation we had not the slightest conception how difficult it is to maintain the peace of the world. And it is difficult because successful international co-operation is no easy task.

We embarked upon World War I with high hopes for the future. We were fighting a war to make the world safe for democracy. On the basis of Wilson's Fourteen Points and the proposed League of Nations, the future peace of the world would be assured.

But the Treaty of Versailles ended in world-wide disillusionment. Cynicism supplanted optimism and hope. And in the interwar period the course of events moved with ups and downs in a direction that reinforced this cynicism.

We embarked upon the present war in an atmosphere wholly different from that of World War I. The young men who were drafted undertook the business at hand with a firm purpose to carry through to the end, but free from unrealistic and superficial illusions. No one could see at all clearly where we were coming out or what would be the solution for the tangled and obstinate problems confronting the modern world. There was no choice. We had to carry on. But there were no illusions about an easy and happy future as we girded ourselves to push through to victory. What lay beyond was by no means clear.

We began the last war with high hopes and ended it in disillusionment; we began this war disillusioned, but as the war moves to a close we emerge in a revival of hope and a growing spirit of confidence—a confidence born of a realistic sifting of the difficulties confronting us.

I believe that there are deep and fundamental reasons why we may expect that the settlement following World War II will rest on a more secure foundation than that which followed World War I. This faith rests not merely in the belief that the terrific experience which has twice confronted this generation has made it less naïve and more realistic. It rests even more upon a constellation of factors that were not planned by human beings—factors that will inevitably and profoundly shape the course of future history. What these factors are in contrast to World War I, I shall elaborate in the course of this chapter.

Why did the settlement following World War I end so disastrously? And is there any firm ground upon which to erect hopes that the prospect following World War II will be any better? To these fundamental questions we must seek an answer in terms both of world politics and of world economics.

The settlement following World War I was doomed to failure for several reasons. World opinion had not yet advanced to a point that made possible even the minimum conditions necessary for the functioning of an international political organization. In the United States we were not even prepared to join the League. There was no general awareness how difficult a matter it is to preserve world peace. Following the Napoleonic Wars, the world had become accustomed to a condition of general peaceful relations, with wars limited to restricted areas, such as the American Civil War and the Franco-Prussian War.

World War I was regarded as an unhappy incident; once finished, it would not be likely, so it was thought, to recur. Large liberal elements in the western democracies had never been convinced that the war was not the product of capitalist and imperialist blundering or, worse yet, contrived with malicious intent. There was no deep feeling that the very existence of the nation was at stake. In the United States, did not perhaps the majority feel that we had unnecessarily been led into a war that did not concern us?

Accordingly, the belief that it was necessary to build an international force to preserve the peace of the world was wholly lacking, at least in the United States. The grave danger of war was not adequately realized. We were prepared to take our chances; we were cynical about our allies; and we drifted on, without knowing it, to the brink of national disaster.

Equally important is the fact that the international political situation in Europe, following World War I, was in an unstable equilibrium. The peace of Versailles was built around France. So built, it failed to take cognizance of stark realities.

Consider France as the cornerstone of the peace settlement. This cornerstone of the new world security was a second-rate power in terms of industrial strength, population and resources. Internally the French nation suffered from deep social and economic cleavages. There was no internal cohesion. There was intense and bitter conflict. Old and outworn patterns of thinking controlled its political and economic policies. The internal problems of France remained unsolved.

Externally France still faced the German giant in the center and heart of Europe. The war had not changed this fundamental fact. This France fully recognized, and her reaction was one of fear. The Maginot line on the west and the ring of buffer states on the east were the external symbols of this fear. But they were no answer to the stark fact that the peace of the world had been erected on too narrow a foundation.

Russia on the other side of the great European giant was an unknown quantity. All the world was skeptical and, indeed, cynical with respect to her political and economic future. Russia remained in greater or less degree an outcast in the family of nations. As such, she could not and did not become a pillar to support the structure of world peace.

England attempted her traditional role of acting as a balance wheel in the constellation of European political forces. But she was bewildered, confused and unable to act. On the one side she wanted to build up a stronger Germany to help promote the economic prosperity of Europe, and on the other she was committed to support, however weakly, the world's peace structure built upon France. She did not know what to make of Russia. As the interwar period wore on, her policies ended in futility and frustration.

We in the United States naïvely believed that Europe could stew in its own juice without danger to our own security. The Atlantic Ocean, it was still believed, was ample protection for the great American continent. We reverted to our agelong isolationism.

World security in the interwar period failed no less because the great industrial nations did not understand and were wholly unprepared to face the economic problems of the postwar world. Everywhere there was an effort to revert to prewar policies and to restore the prewar economy. This effort failed. Price fluctuations in all countries, inflation in Germany and France, a persistent core of unemployment in England, increasing disequilibrium in the primary-producing countries, boom and depression in the United States—these were the manifestations of economic unbalance all over the world.

All hopes for the restoration of the prewar economy were dashed in the great depression. International economic co-operation was completely cast aside. Each nation struggled by whatever means it could grasp to stay above water. Economic warfare became the rule. Tariff increases, import quotas, exchange control, competitive exchange depreciation, bilateralism and multiple currencies destroyed multilateral trade and the international price system.

Could we have stopped the great depression dead in its tracks and gone on to high levels of income and employment and rising standards of living throughout the world, we might eventually have rebuilt the structure of world peace on firmer foundations. But the great depression fanned the flames of a new world conflagration. It required four years of mass unemployment to bring Hitler to power in Germany. The reabsorption of these unemployed into war industries and into the army and navy solved for Germany at one and the same time the problem of unemployment and the problem of revitalized military power. Confused and distracted by the problems of the depression, the growing menace of Germany was not faced by western Europe and the United States. Russia alone, insulated by her economic system from the ravages of the world-wide cumulative deflation, had the strength and the insight to face the new menace and to prepare for resistance.

International co-operation thus failed after World War I, first because of the unstable political equilibrium in Europe and second because of the uncontrolled or uncontrollable economic disaster which engulfed the world in the decade of the thirties.

What, now, are the prospects after World War II? A great new fact emerges from World War II. It will change the face of Europe. It will profoundly dominate the course of world history in the generations that lie before us.

This great new fact is the rise of Russia on one side of the globe and the economic and military power of the United States on the other. A happy geographical accident—two great powers occupying vast continents and controlling vast resources in areas that are noncompetitive—this fact must be set down as a dominating and directing force in the future course of history. We are confronted here with a completely new constellation of forces. Within this framework the role of France, Germany and England of necessity must be something very different from that set by the European patterns of past generations.

This new constellation of forces presents, one may believe, a realistic hope for a new basis for world security and world peace. It does not rest mainly upon the frailties of human good will and good intentions but on a rock-bottom geographical fact. Here is a framework within which international co-operation has a chance to succeed. World security and world peace rest basically upon the United States and Russia. These two great powers must co-operate with other countries, large and small, to secure world peace, and the co-operation must take concrete form in a United Nations international organization.

In between those two powers on opposite sides of the globe is the British Empire which emerges from World War II *abso-lutely* stronger than ever before. As such it can act as a powerful cementing and balancing factor. With respect to the European sphere, the United Kingdom can be greatly reinforced, in this balancing role, by the countries of western Europe. On the other side of the globe, China and the British Empire can play an equally balancing role. Here are solid pillars upon which a United Nations and ultimately a truly international security organization can be built.

Germany at the end of World War II will be confronted with an entirely new world: on the one side the crushing might of a new Russia and on the other the demonstrated power of the United States and the British Empire. A generation hence Russia will have a population of over 250 million; her industrial strength and her productive power will have increased several-fold. A generation hence Russia will loom up as a great colossus. Confronted with this giant in terms both of population and of industrial development Germany cannot again challenge the peace of the world.

We are thus confronted with a new political equilibrium following World War II. But what about the world economic situation? Are we better prepared to meet our economic problems than we were after World War I?

Here again, I think, there is solid ground not indeed for optimism but for hope. There can be no question that a profound revolution has occurred in economic thinking throughout the world. We have learned a great deal from the experiences of the last two decades. In the United States we have introduced a number of important reforms which will tend to minimize the distortions of a boom period. And we are not hopelessly at sea, as we were in 1929, with respect to ways and means of heading off a rapidly cumulating depression. For example, the crazy financing of home mortgages prevalent in the twenties created a thoroughly unsound situation which intensified the collapse that followed. This situation has now been remedied through the reforms instituted under the Federal Housing Administration. Reforms relating to the stock market, including the Securities Exchange Commission and margin regulations, tend to prevent such unhealthy speculation as prevailed in the twenties. Important banking reforms have been instituted, including the guarantee of deposits. The social-security program puts a floor under depressions. These and many other measures help to remove artificial distortions and to minimize the danger of unchecked collapse following a boom.

Even more important is the fact that we have definitely abandoned the view that a depression must be allowed to run its course. While it cannot be claimed that we have developed any far-reaching program that assures the mastery of our economic fate, nevertheless marked progress has been made. I do not think that any future administration in the United States would again sit idly by while the national income falls rapidly to half its former level as occurred from 1929 to 1932. We have learned ways and means of stopping such a catastrophic development. We are no longer hampered by the doubts, fears and restraints that prevented us then from taking vigorous action. All this represents a major gain.

Throughout the world, leaders in government and in industry are more and more committed to a program of sustained full employment. This does not mean that anyone believes that perfection can be achieved. We shall fall short of the goal aimed at. There will be fluctuations in employment. But we are determined, through antidepression measures, to moderate these fluctuations. All modern governments are increasingly committed to expansionist and developmental programs, to the promotion of rising standards of living and to the creation of underlying conditions necessary for the attainment of full employment.

A new attitude, moreover, is prevalent among the leading industrial countries with respect to the primary-producing and economically backward countries. In former times these retarded countries throughout the world were condemned to the position of economic colonies. They were mere appendages to the economies of the great industrial nations. Economic policies were as a matter of course directed toward the continuance of the status of economic colonialism. The industrially backward countries were expected to supply raw materials for the great countries and, in turn, to furnish a market for manufactured products.

There is a new outlook abroad in the world today. Now, everywhere the note is sounded that development, diversification and industrialization must be undertaken in the backward areas. We have come to realize that the future trade of the world cannot continue to run in the simplified terms of exchange of raw materials for finished manufactured products.

Rather, it must run in terms of highly diversified trade between countries with different skills and resources but each developed to the fullest possible extent. Large-scale developmental projects, industrialization to an extent that is economically feasible, and the diversification of agriculture; the development and improvement of human resources through improved health, nutrition and education; the promotion of a higher standard of living, rising productivity, and increased purchasing power—these are the new world economic goals. They promise a more stable economy and better living standards everywhere.

A beginning has already been made to instrument these international policies. We are in process of setting up a United Nations Organization on Food and Agriculture designed to increase agricultural efficiency and nutritional standards throughout the world. Articles of Agreement were reached by the delegates of 44 nations at Bretton Woods on an International Bank for Reconstruction and Development. The proposed Bank for Reconstruction and Development is a symbol of the new world outlook. Development, diversification, industrialization and expansion—these are the ideas that underly the concept of the International Bank.

In more and more countries definite monetary and fiscal programs are being developed to promote full employment and economic stability. The automatic processes upon which we still relied after World War I have been found wanting. Between the two wars more and more countries have set up central banks and improved their monetary and banking structures. In place of the automatic gold standard, international monetary co-operation is everywhere recognized as a necessary condition for an orderly world. Such co-operation is already under way and must assume concrete embodiment in institutional arrangements of some kind. The International

Monetary Fund proposed at Bretton Woods is a carefully thought-out plan designed to meet present-day international monetary needs.

Other international conferences dealing with commercial policy, air routes, oil, cartels and commodity agreements are under way. It is apparent that the leading countries of the world are far more aware of the basic importance of economic problems in international relations, and see far more realistically now than before what these basic economic problems are.

Thus there is, I believe, a realistic basis for a hopeful view of the future, in terms both of the new international political equilibrium and of the guiding principles of economic policy which increasingly dominate thinking throughout the world.

But it would be a great mistake to think that the problems of the future are easy ones or that the future is in any sense secure. I repeat, it will be no easy matter to maintain the peace of the world. Fortunate as the geographical position of the United States and Russia is, innumerable frictions will tend to develop between us not only with respect to the problems of Germany and western Europe but also those of the Far East. Eternal vigilance and the utmost good will are needed. Unless we realize the difficulty of the task and the dangers that lurk on every hand, we shall not remain alert and prepared to play our role in international co-operation.

Equally, the economic problems that confront us in both the domestic sphere and the international sphere are infinitely complex and difficult. We have as yet only reached the kindergarten stage in learning how to manage our complex economic problems. But we have made a beginning. We have freed ourselves in large measure from the restraints that formerly tied us hand and foot and made it impossible to act. We are increasingly developing the tools and mechanisms needed for the task. But we have yet to work out a comprehensive, far-reaching program both on the domestic front and the international, adequate to give us confidence and faith that our economic future is secure.

CHAPTER II

THE ECONOMIC BASIS OF
SOUND INTERNATIONAL RELATIONS

I HAVE the strong impression that many persons vitally interested in sound international relations are too frequently disposed to assume that a high level of economic prosperity in all countries would be assured if trade barriers were largely removed. It is undoubtedly true that the erection of postwar agricultural tariffs, together with the increasingly protectionist policies of many countries, the reparation payments, and the unsound policies pursued with respect to foreign lending, were important factors intensifying the terrific world depression beginning in 1929. While this may certainly be granted, it would be a great mistake to assume that sounder international economic policies of the character referred to above would themselves insure an avoidance of serious depressions. Indeed, one can go much farther and assert that even in a world that was completely under one political sovereignty the fundamental factor producing depressions would still be present, namely, the fluctuation in the volume of real investment.[1]

In laying plans for a durable peace it would be very dangerous to overlook the threat to the stability of any arrangements

[1] See my article in International Conciliation Bulletin, April, 1941.

that may be made should we experience a recurrence of deep depressions.

I think it is increasingly the view of economists that the depression starting in 1929 is in very large measure responsible for the present plight of the world. There was a very good chance—though no absolute certainty—that in the absence of the great depression a solution might have been found for the central problem of Europe, namely, the place of Germany in international relations. Despite the mistakes of the Versailles Treaty, progress was being made toward a solution in the relatively prosperous years of the late twenties, and could this prosperity have been maintained on a fairly high level, it is not unreasonable to assume that, progressively, a solution would have been found and war thereby averted.

The thesis can, therefore, be advanced with a good deal of reason that the really acid test of international economic cooperation runs in terms of deliberate international policy with respect to the control or moderation of depressions.

With respect to the United States, it may be asserted with a good deal of confidence that this country could make no greater contribution toward the solution of the international political as well as economic problems than that of achieving a high degree of internal economic stability at a level of fairly full employment of labor and other resources. It is, I think, a fact that the extraordinary instability of the American economy presents one of the most serious problems confronting Europe and, indeed, the whole world. The great depression itself was, of course, a result of the interplay of a great many factors, partly internal and partly international, but there can be little question that the tremendous investment boom of the twenties in the United States (and in other countries fostered by American foreign loans), the succeeding high degree of temporary saturation and the ensuing collapse in the output of fixed capital goods, particularly in this country, were the central core of the great world depression and determined in the main its intensity and duration. A bad international setup, of course, magnified the impact upon the outside world, and this impact in turn reflected itself back upon our own country in a cumulative fashion. Thus, as always in a depression period, it is quite impossible to unravel the interplay of cause and effect relationships. But through it all it is important to see the internal situation in the United States which would have created a profound depression regardless of the international setup.

Europe, and the primary-producing countries as well, from whom we import so heavily and whose prosperity or depression is, therefore, in large measure a reflection of our own, have every reason to fear the impact of America upon world affairs if we continue a high degree of economic instability or chronically depressed conditions as in the interwar years.

It is a striking fact that the movements of the Federal Reserve index of industrial production in the last decades bear a close resemblance to the movements in the quantum of world trade. A sharp depression in the United States spreads to the rest of the world through the sudden decline in American imports induced by our depression. A low rate of activity in America inevitably throws the American trade and service payments on international account into disequilibrium. A violently fluctuating American economy is a menace to economic stability in the rest of the world. A chronically depressed America, unless the world can in some manner isolate itself from this depressional influence, tends to infect other countries.

Under these circumstances it is highly probable that unless the United States can do a better job of managing its own economy and can effectively co-operate with other countries on monetary policy, fiscal policy, and on a co-ordinated international program of expansion and development to combat depression and unemployment, it will become necessary for foreign countries to insulate themselves as far as possible from the American influence. It is by no means improbable that without an adequate internal American policy, combined with international collaboration along the lines indicated, the European countries will find it essential to their political and economic stability to collaborate on policies designed to segregate themselves economically from the United States. This would indeed be a world tragedy.

Through management of the exchange rate and other controls elaborated during the period of the war, it is not improbable that there might be integrated into a fairly unified system a considerable international area, including not only the British Empire and the countries of western Europe but also at least that section of Latin America whose trade has always been closely linked with England and western Europe. Such a quasi-union would embrace a very considerable part of the modern industrial world. But with the United States left out we should have world chaos.

All countries are aware of the economic difficulties that will confront them at the end of the war, particularly the danger of mass unemployment. In addition to political reconstruction, bold economic and financial planning on a world-wide scale is required, involving international developmental projects and internal domestic programs to promote high levels of production and rising living standards. International collaboration with respect to internal expansion within each country must, moreover, be undertaken with a view to the promotion of international equilibrium.

In an article in the *New Statesman and Nation* written as early as February 17, 1940, reference was made to the perilous situation that will confront all the belligerent countries when the armies are demobilized and returned to civilian life. The worst error, it was urged, committed by the statesmen following World War I was not the Treaty of Versailles with its doubtful political frontiers, but rather their failure to grapple effectively with the economics of the postwar world. The first chapter in peace settlement ought to include an ambitious plan of international reconstruction and developmental programs combined with internal policies to maintain full employment.

Undoubtedly, intelligent opinion throughout the world eagerly hopes and plans for international collaboration with the United States. But this is true only on the assumption that there is reason to suppose that the United States can and will stabilize its economy at a high employment level and that it can and will participate in effective international collaboration along monetary, trade and fiscal lines.

What I have tried to state briefly is my conviction that it is necessary to think of international economic co-operation in more thoroughgoing terms than has commonly been the case. It is important not merely to think in terms of the optimum international division of labor which at full employment would give us the largest realizable real income. In the kind of world in which we live today it is even more important to realize how difficult the goal of full employment is and to consider those domestic and international policies that will tend to promote this end.

CHAPTER III

THE NEED FOR
INTERNATIONAL ECONOMIC CO-OPERATION

World Instability in the Interwar Period, 1919–39

THE WORLD as a whole failed miserably to make the economy function in a satisfactory manner in the two decades between the two world wars. For this the great industrial nations that control the bulk of the world's resources are mainly to blame. By failing to make adequate use of their own resources in the interest of their own people, economic distress spread to the countries less adequately endowed with natural resources. Out of this failure sprang the breakdown of the world economy and indeed of international political security.

Between the two world wars, we suffered, throughout the western world with varying degrees in different countries, violent price fluctuations, catastrophic movements in the level of production, prolonged intervals of mass unemployment in all the major industrial countries, and very serious undermining of property values, leading in some countries to widespread bankruptcy and in others to a virtual elimination of the middle class.

We shall not succeed in establishing a secure political world following this war unless we solve our economic problems. High levels of employment and a high degree of economic stability underlie, basically, all programs of international relations. Unless these economic ends are achieved, any United Nations program along political lines will utterly fail. It would be suicidal to assume that these economic ends can be expected to be reached by letting things take their course.

Accordingly, there is a growing belief throughout the world that a number of new international economic institutions must be undertaken, and that all nations must earnestly co-operate to secure enlightened management of these institutions so that they may contribute to the desired economic goals of stability and full employment.

That international economic relations had reached a serious impasse by September, 1939, is fully evident from the growth of bilateralism, clearing agreements and foreign-exchange control.

The reconstruction of a multilateral trade system will obviously encounter serious obstacles. To begin with, there is the current maldistribution of international monetary reserves evidenced by the fact that the United States now holds $21 billion worth of gold, nearly two-thirds of the world's supply of monetary gold. It is true that the abnormal holdings by the United States do not necessarily imply that foreign countries are possessed of insufficient reserves to operate a free-exchange system. Foreign countries outside of the United States hold about $14 billions of gold which exceeds by 50 per cent the total gold (dollar value) held by all countries in the world in 1925. Moreover, new gold production is now enormously greater than in the twenties and this also must be taken into account. The gold holdings of foreign countries are, however, not well distributed among the different countries nor do all countries participate at all equally in the new gold production.

It is also true that the abnormal gold inflow into the United States in the thirties was related not solely or even mainly to a world disequilibrium in the current international account but largely to capital movements. Thus, of the $16 billion worth of gold inflow (1934–42), $6 billion may be attributable to an export surplus (heavy in the years 1939, 1940 and 1941), while the remaining $10 billion are attributable either to recorded capital inflow ($6 billion) or to unidentified transactions ($4 billion). Of the capital inflow, about $2 billion represented return of American capital, about $½ billion foreign purchase of American securities and about $1½ billion increased balances of central banks and governments in the United States. A considerable amount of the capital inflow clearly represented "hot money," and the whole was more or less related to disturbed political conditions. Thus factors other than the "chronic world shortage of dollars" have been responsible for the larger part of the heavy gold inflow into the United States.

World Shortage of Dollars

But apart from the political and other factors, the United States has tended over many years to drain a disproportionate share of the world's gold owing to underlying economic factors affecting its current international account.

Related to this chronic disequilibrium is the long-run tendency through several decades of the terms of trade (i. e., the ratio of export prices to import prices) to move against the agricultural and raw-material countries. This tendency, basically resting upon the relatively inelastic demand for most agricultural products and coupled with the increasing diversification of consumption and higher standards of living in the advanced countries, has caused the demand for agricultural products to fall in relation to that for industrial products. A rapidly developing agricultural technique (increasing agricultural efficiency and productivity) confronted by an inelastic demand schedule compels either serious deterioration of the terms of trade for these countries or emigration of their population or their transfer into industry in their own country. The net effect in fact has been partly deterioration of the terms of trade and partly an accentuation of industrialization.

The drastic redistribution of international assets (Germany in the last war and England in World War II) accentuates the international disequilibrium. Britain, having largely lost her net-creditor position and having suffered a substantial deterioration in her exports, must nevertheless import foodstuffs and raw materials to prevent a decline in her standard of living. Britain is, moreover, unable to compete with the United States in just those products in greatest demand as living standards rise—automobiles, radios, phonographs, typewriters, electrical appliances and the like. The technical superiority of the United States, the unfavorable terms of trade in the agricultural and raw-material countries, and the drastic redistribution of international assets combine to create a continued disequilibrium in world trade.

Means of Achieving International Balance

The main means to achieve international equilibrium are (a) the promotion of full employment in the industrially mature countries, and especially in the United States, (b) the development and industrialization of the backward countries designed to change the structure of their economies, and (c) a liberalization of commercial and tariff policies throughout the world, and notably in the United States.

International collaboration to secure full employment in the industrially mature countries promotes international equilibrium in the respect that a full-employment income in these countries tends to spread prosperity throughout the world and in general promotes a high level of world trade. Within the framework of full employment and a high level of world trade, substantial tariff reductions become feasible, and price adjustments incident to changes in the United States tariffs and exchange rates can be more effective than is possible under conditions of underemployment.

A structural change in the economies of undeveloped countries is equally important. This means diversification of agriculture, better equipment on farms, mechanization of agricultural production, improved transportation facilities, electrification and the spread of industrialization. Industrialization is typically possible along the following lines: (a) the first stages in the processing of indigenous raw materials, (b) the development of lighter consumer-goods industries and (c) the assembling of complicated industrial products manufactured abroad. Diversification and industrialization, moreover, require the promotion of large-scale developmental projects, including electric power, port facilities, river-valley development, roads, railroads, airways and other communications. Thus the basic solution runs in terms of the spread of capital equipment and modern techniques throughout the world.

In order to effectuate the necessary programs of adjustment it will be necessary to engage in international economic co-operation on many fronts. Some of the more important of these institutions will be discussed in the following pages.

PART TWO

THE ECONOMIC FOUNDATIONS
OF WORLD SECURITY

CHAPTER IV

THE INTERNATIONAL BANK FOR
RECONSTRUCTION AND DEVELOPMENT

FORTY-FOUR nations participated in the Monetary and Financial Conference at Bretton Woods in July, 1944. The Conference reached agreement on two far-reaching proposals designed to promote postwar international progress and stability. I propose to discuss the Bretton Woods Agreements on an International Bank for Reconstruction and Development and on the International Monetary Fund in the five following chapters.

Character and Functions of the Bank

What is the nature of the International Bank for Reconstruction and Development? How will it function? What results can it be expected to achieve? How will it affect the interests of American investors, American exporters, American labor and American farmers? How will it affect the prosperity of the United States? How will it affect world economic stability?

The Bank is expected to aid reconstruction in war-devastated countries and to promote economic development in backward countries.

The Bank will have a capital of $9.1 billion subscribed to by member countries. The capital subscription assigned to each member corresponds roughly to its relative size and importance in the world economy. The share assigned to the United States is $3,175 million. Only 10 per cent of the subscription is to be paid in at the outset, the remainder being subject to call.

Including the 10 per cent initially called in, the Bank has the power to call up to a maximum of 20 per cent of the capital for direct loans to foreign countries or foreign enterprises. In this case the Bank would make loans from its own capital funds. It is, however, doubtful that the Bank will use, except in rare cases, its own capital funds for direct loans. The Bank will be essentially an underwriting and guaranteeing institution. It will, in the usual case, guarantee issues floated by foreign borrowers in the private-capital markets. The Bank may also, if this is deemed desirable, issue its own bonds in the private-capital markets, and from the funds so raised make direct loans to foreign borrowers.

To sum up, the Bank may (a) make direct loans from its own capital, (b) make direct loans from funds raised in the private-capital markets through the issue of its own bonds and (c) guarantee issues placed by foreign borrowers in the private-capital markets.

High-grade Bonds

The total volume of direct loans together with the total volume of guaranteed loans may not exceed the total subscribed capital and accumulated reserves of the Bank. Thus the total liabilities that may be incurred cannot exceed the capital resources of the Bank, and thus the total maximum risk which any member country undertakes in joining the Bank is limited to its subscribed capital. At the very worst (assuming the loans proved to be a total loss—a wholly unrealistic assumption) the United States could not lose as a maximum more than its subscription.

Since the loans and guarantees are backed 100 per cent by the capital of the Bank, over and above the guarantee of the borrowing country, the bonds issued or guaranteed by the

Bank must be regarded as very high-grade, gilt-edged securities. It can be assumed that they would be regarded in the investment markets as among the best securities in the world.

Bank Supplements Private Lending

The Bank does not supplant private international lending and private international investment. No borrowing country can use the Bank if it can float loans at reasonable rates. The Bank will, however, enable productive development projects to be undertaken in countries that could not borrow on reasonable terms without the aid of the Bank.

Why an *international* Bank since, in fact, most of the money must come from the United States? Why should we not continue the Export-Import Bank? Why cannot private international lending do the job? How can an international bank make sound and economic loans if, in fact, these loans are not sufficiently profitable to induce private lending? Will not the Bank in fact compete with and even supplant private international lending?

Bank Similar to the Federal Housing Administration

To answer these questions it is vitally important to see clearly and precisely what the International Bank for Reconstruction and Development is. It can, in fact, be described as essentially a mutual loan insurance and guaranty institution.

Consider the F.H.A. by way of comparison. The average American citizen by now understands fairly well how the F.H.A. functions. It has aptly been described as a system of mutual mortgage insurance. Under the F.H.A. a prospective home owner who wishes to build a new house may apply for an F.H.A. mortgage. The purchaser of the mortgage—the lender—may be a commercial bank, a savings bank, an insurance company or some other financial institution. The money loaned is therefore not government money but represents private savings and the funds of private financial institutions.

The borrower engages to pay the lender not only the interest but also an insurance premium of one-half of 1 per cent. This insurance premium is paid into a central pool administered by the F.H.A. and is the second line of defense (the first line of defense being, of course, the house itself against which the mortgage is placed) protecting investors in home mortgages all over the United States. The third and ultimate line of defense is the guarantee of the United States Treasury which is the final and complete protection for the investor.

Here is a system of mutual mortgage insurance with a final guarantee by the government. It is a system brilliantly contrived to tap private savings and investment funds for home construction with a minimum of government activity. The central insurance pool could not, of course, be established without some centralizing agency such as the F.H.A. And there would be no assurance that the mortgages, even with this central pool, would prove an entirely safe investment without the ultimate underwriting of the federal treasury.

The International Bank for Reconstruction and Development will operate in the international lending field precisely in the manner described above with respect to the financing under the F.H.A. program of home mortgages in the United States. As in the case of the prospective home owner, the foreign borrower (whether national government, municipality or private corporation) will apply to the Bank for the insurance and guarantee of a loan. The foreign government or foreign corporation will float its bonds, say in the capital markets of the United States. These bond issues will be insured and guaranteed by the International Bank.

The borrower will engage to pay not only the interest on

the bond but also "an insurance premium" (in the Bretton Woods Agreement called a commission charge) of 1 to 1½ per cent, precisely as the home borrower engages to pay interest plus an insurance premium. The insurance premiums paid by all foreign borrowers utilizing the facilities of the Bank will accumulate in a central pool administered by the Bank and will serve, as in the case of the F.H.A., as a second line of defense protecting the lender. The first line of defense, of course, is the value or assets of the project against which the loan is made, together with (as explicitly provided in the Bank statutes) the guarantee of the national government of the country in which the loan is made. The third and ultimate line of defense is the guarantee by the International Bank itself. This guarantee is backed up by the capital of the Bank.

The capital of the Bank is subscribed to at agreed-upon quotas by all the member countries. The only difference between the Bank and the F.H.A. guarantee is that the Treasury underwriting of the F.H.A. loans is unlimited, whereas the underwriting by the various countries of the international loans is limited to their capital subscriptions to the Bank. The underwriting, despite this limitation, is nevertheless thoroughly good, since the volume of loans that may be underwritten cannot exceed the total subscribed capital of the Bank. Thus while the guarantee is limited to the subscribed quota of each country, on the other hand, the volume of loans that may be guaranteed is limited by the same amount. The guarantee is therefore dollar for dollar equal to the maximum volume of loans that may be made.

Thus in all respects the International Bank functions in a manner closely analogous to the functioning of the F.H.A. It is a system of mutual loan insurance in which the borrower pays an insurance premium to a centralized pool and the whole is ultimately underwritten by the guarantee of the contributing governments up to the amount of their subscribed capital in the Bank.

How Much Will It Cost?

In the case of the F.H.A., the Treasury has not been called upon to make any appropriation to furnish loans to home builders; the money comes from private sources. Nor has any appropriation been made to guarantee or underwrite the loans. It is true that in passing the Federal Housing Administration Act, Congress undertook a potential liability in the event that the losses of the F.H.A. mortgage system should exceed the accumulated resources of the insurance pool.

In substantially similar fashion the International Bank will involve no appropriation by Congress except the capital paid in at the outset amounting to 10 per cent of the total subscribed. Of this 10 per cent, however, only 2 per cent must be paid in gold, and the remaining 8 per cent may be paid in currency or a noninterest-bearing obligation. Of the remaining 90 per cent of the subscribed capital another 10 per cent may be called if the Bank wishes to use its own capital funds to make direct loans. This, however, is on the whole unlikely, so that the remaining 90 per cent will not require an appropriation by Congress unless the international loans underwritten and guaranteed by the Bank prove to encounter losses that cannot be covered by the central insurance pool. Only in this event would further appropriation of funds by Congress become necessary.

Thus in the first instance the establishment of the Bank calls for an appropriation of 10 per cent of our subscribed capital or $317.5 million, of which $63.5 million would be paid in gold and the remaining $254 million in currency or a noninterest demand note. Authorization, however, for the ultimate possible liability of $3,175 million would, of course, be made upon congressional approval of the Agreement.

Reforms Needed in International Lending Field

There is thus a close analogy between the International Bank and the F.H.A. home-mortgage system. There are many ways in which it may be expected that the operation of the Bank in the international sphere may have results comparable to those which the F.H.A. has achieved in the home-mortgage market.

Prior to the establishment of the F.H.A., home-mortgage financing in the United States was in a deplorably chaotic and unsound condition. Not only was there a wide differential in the various regions of the United States in interest rates on first mortgages but in addition in many sections of the country second and third mortgages, with exorbitant and even usurious rates, were piled on top. The height of the average interest rate, first, second and third mortgage combined, was such that default by the borrower might almost be said to be invited and, in fact, in a large proportion of cases was rendered inevitable. In addition, however, the financing was undertaken typically without any provision for amortization whatever, and in other cases with wholly inadequate provision for amortization. This was the second widespread cause of defaults. In the third place, loans were made without adequate (if indeed any) appraisal analysis of the burden undertaken by the borrower in relation to his capacity to pay. In the fourth place no adequate standards were enforced by the mortgage lenders on the quality and soundness of the construction or on the quality of the materials used. It was a period of jerry-building.

The conditions obtaining with respect to home mortgages in the United States prior to the advent of the F.H.A. constitute almost a perfect description of the deplorable conditions that existed with respect to international lending particularly in the boom twenties. The interest rates and commissions charged were so high as to invite default. Amortization was typically not provided for. The loans were frequently made without adequate study and appraisal of specific projects and, indeed, in many cases were made without reference to the uses to which the loans would be put. Thus investment bankers were known to approach foreign governments with the offer of a loan and even urged them to increase the loan without regard to the manner in which the funds were expended. Interested primarily in their underwriting and commission earnings there was no adequate protection provided for the ultimate investor on the one side or for safeguarding the interests of the borrower on the other. Thus the international lending was conducted on an even worse plane than the home-mortgage lending in the United States. In the case of the latter, the lender at any rate made a loan on a specific project, though the project was inadequately appraised and inadequate construction standards were applied. In international lending, however, frequently the loans were made without any reference to any productive project whatever and therefore could only be regarded at best as speculative or, still worse, as simply throwing money away to spendthrift and irresponsible borrowers.

Just as the F.H.A. has brought order and sound common sense into the home-mortgage field and has lifted the standards of the home-mortgage market, affording protection to both borrower and lender, so the International Bank may be expected to regularize and improve the standards of international lending.

Under the terms of the Bank statutes, the Bank may not underwrite, insure or guarantee a loan except on specific projects and not until a thorough study of the proposal has been made by a competent committee of technical experts. This committee must report on the productive character of the project, its probable effect upon the real income and development of the country, its contribution to the wealth and resources of the country, together with the probable beneficial effect of the project upon the international balance of payment position of the country in question. This sets a new standard for international lending. The statutes of the Bank, moreover, provide that the schedule for repayment of the principal shall be appropriate to the project. Suitable provision for amortization is thus made. Finally, the fact that the borrower will be afforded the benefit of low, gilt-edged interest rates, plus a moderate and reasonable insurance premium (commission charge) of 1 to 1½ per cent, contributes in no inconsiderable degree to the ultimate soundness of the loan in that the charges will be within reach of the capacity of the borrower to pay.

Under the functioning of the International Bank the wide diversity of rates charged in different parts of the world will tend to diminish, just as has occurred under the operation of the F.H.A. with respect to home mortgages. International lending will thus be placed all around on a sounder and less discriminatory basis than it has been in the past. The effect of the International Bank upon international lending will promote higher standards and will serve to protect the interests of both borrower and lender in a manner very similar to the achievements of the F.H.A. in the domestic home-mortgage field.

CHAPTER V

CRITICISMS OF THE INTERNATIONAL BANK

THE BRETTON WOODS proposal to set up an International Bank for Reconstruction and Development has been subjected to numerous criticisms. These criticisms deserve careful consideration. No plan should be adopted without careful and thoroughgoing scrutiny of the plan as a whole and of its separate details.

Why Not an American Bank?

The criticism most frequently made against the Bank is that there is no need for such an international institution. It is not denied that international loans need to be made. Many critics agree, moreover, that the government needs to play a role in order to insure an adequate volume of international loans. It is argued, however, that the funds must of necessity come mainly from the United States. If this is so, why, then, should the lending take place through an international institution? Why not use an enlarged American Export-Import Bank to make international loans? [1]

The first answer to this criticism runs in terms of our own self-interest. It is true that most of the bonds guaranteed or issued by the International Bank for Reconstruction and Development will be floated in the capital markets of the United States. It is true that American investors will furnish most of the funds. Nevertheless, it is to our own self-interest to participate in the establishment of an International Bank. This is true because under the Bank proposal the bonds purchased by American citizens will be guaranteed and underwritten not merely by our own government but by all the governments of the world as well. Our government, in fact, will shoulder approximately a third of the risk. Surely it is to our interest that our government should shoulder only a third of the risk rather than the whole of the risk. About this there could scarcely be any difference of opinion.

It is, however, argued that in terms of our own self-interest we could control the terms of the lending to our own export

[1] See my essay in *International Financial Stabilization, a Symposium*, published by the Irving Trust Company, New York, December, 1944.

advantage if we made the loans through a purely American institution. It is argued, for example, that we could insist that all borrowers buy machinery and other equipment in the American market.

Let us examine this argument. This country has had much to say in recent years about the evils of bilateral deals such as those made by Nazi Germany. These Nazi deals could be forced upon countries by Germany because of their urgent need to export to Germany. In like manner if the United States loaned exclusively through its own Export-Import Bank, it would be in a position to compel purchases of capital goods in our market in return for the privilege of borrowing American capital.

The Nazi German sales were not based on the quality and price of German products; they were forced upon the foreign country by economic necessity. In similar manner, under the suggested plan our sales of machinery would not be based on superior quality or lower price but on coercion. If the foreign countries will not buy here, they cannot borrow here.

Such trading methods may in the short run appear advantageous, but in the long run they will not endure. Foreign countries operating under such coercion will resent it and will attempt at the earliest possible moment to make arrangements with other countries wherever this is feasible; and there are other countries with which they can make deals.

Canada has developed enormous industrial capacity and is eagerly looking for foreign markets. Sweden, Switzerland and Australia would also be able to supply industrial exports immediately after the war. And it will not be long before France, England and even Germany will be in the market. In the meantime the coercive practices of the United States, followed by discriminatory competitive retaliations from other exporting countries, would have done the cause of international good will, world stability and economic progress great harm.

American industries need, in fact, have no fear in a free and nondiscriminatory market. There is not the slightest question that the borrowing country, left quite free to buy wherever it wishes, will, in fact, buy very heavily from the United States. Our machine industries are and will continue to be in the forefront in a world of free and open competition. And to the extent that the borrowing countries buy machinery elsewhere, whenever quality or price so directs, the increased prosperity of the exporting country will, in turn, promote their purchases from the United States. Thus in the long run there can be no question that the sound policy—the one that both engenders good will and that brings our industries contented and continuing customers—is the one that rests on multilateral trade, free and open competition, nondiscriminatory and noncoercive practices.

Continued Role of American Export-Import Bank

The establishment of an International Bank for Reconstruction and Development does not mean, however, that the United States must liquidate the American Export-Import Bank. Within the framework of international collaboration the American Export-Import Bank can play an important role. It will do so mainly in the financing of intermediate credit for the benefit of our exporters. But it may also from time to time, in consultation with the International Bank, make long-term loans. Loans may be made, for example, to Latin-American countries in the event that such loans are mutually beneficial to the foreign country and to the United States and in no way interfere with a sound international program. Indeed, the International Bank for Reconstruction and Development is eager to be a lender of last resort, to use its resources for productive and basic developments which cannot otherwise be financed on reasonable terms. Private lending is welcomed to the utmost and, equally, lending by the American Export-Import Bank whenever such lending is consistent with our international commitments and with a genuinely international program.

Bank under Debtor-Country Control

The objection is sometimes raised against the Bank that if our foreign investments are made through it, we cannot effectively control the use of the funds and insure that the funds will not be wasted by the borrower. It is alleged that the Bank will be largely under the control of the borrowing countries and that therefore the creditor countries will, in fact, be in a weak position to protect their loans.

This criticism fails to take cognizance of the temper of the modern world. It is not unlike the view held predominantly some decades past (and even now in a restricted circle of employers) with respect to labor relations. It is, however, increasingly recognized that collective bargaining is the only way to manage the modern labor problem. Similarly, it is more and more coming to be recognized that international consultation and good will are the only way to insure the validity of international contracts.

From this standpoint a very good case could be made out to change over the American Export-Import Bank into an Inter-American Bank. Such an Inter-American Bank would in no wise change the fundamental fact that the United States is the country that furnishes the funds and that the other countries are the borrowers. It would, however, remove any possible argument that the United States was playing Shylock. An Inter-American Bank would promote self-discipline among the members and would relieve the United States from alone carrying the onus of securing enforcement of contract. We know from past experience that countries have not hesitated to default on bonds issued in the American private-capital market.

To be sure, they are likely to be more reluctant to default on loans made by the American Export-Import Bank. And, indeed, the record of these loans is incontestable. They would be still more reluctant to default on bonds that they and their neighbors help to underwrite. International collaboration is a sound training school for self-discipline and higher standards of financial performance.

Why Not Leave It to Private Bankers?

Another criticism directed at the Bank is that a private institution comprising leading American banks could do the job just as well as a governmental institution.

This argument overlooks two fundamental points. In the first place an International Bank can secure the collaboration and guarantee of the borrowing country and its utmost good faith to a degree that is not possible with respect to private lenders. But there is a more important consideration. The view that anything that may be done on a sound basis by government can equally be done on a sound basis by private financing institutions completely overlooks one of the most fundamental considerations with respect to public investment in general. The private lending and guaranteeing institution can only undertake such projects as offer a high assurance of profit on the venture in question. Governments (underwriting an international loan) can look beyond the direct return to the general effect of the project in question upon the prosperity of their economies as a whole and upon the world economy. Governments, in short, can look to both the direct and indirect effects of any project. The guaranteeing governments can, therefore, afford to take a larger risk than could private financial institutions. This does not mean that they will not be prudent in making their investments. It does mean that governments can support basic development projects upon which other profitable developments rest but which themselves may be relatively un-profitable.

The governments participating in the International Bank can support basic development projects (such as roads, port facilities, river-valley developments, large-scale agricultural development programs) which in whole or in part are not self-liquidating. The International Bank can afford to assume such risk if the basic projects, taking all their ramifications into account, are productive and profitable from the standpoint of the indirect effect upon the economy of the borrowing country as a whole and more generally upon world prosperity and world trade.

This in no sense means that private lending and private investment will not continue to play an important and significant role wherever the projects do afford a prospect for direct profitability. Whenever loans can be made on reasonable terms, private lending will do the job. The Bank Agreement specifically provides that it will not make or guarantee a loan if foreign governments or foreign private undertakings can obtain loans on reasonable terms without going to the Bank.

The Bank supplements—it does not supplant—private foreign loans and investments. It is not a competitor. Indeed, it can reasonably be expected that projects undertaken by the Bank will open up new outlets for profitable private investment.

No private financial institution could undertake, for instance, so vast and uncertain a project as the comprehensive development of the Tennessee or Columbia River valleys. Yet these projects promote productivity and business expansion in these regions and throughout the United States. The development of the resources of these regions encourages new industries and increases the markets for all private business. These examples, drawn from our domestic economy, illustrate the role that the International Bank can play in the world economy.

CHAPTER VI

THE INTERNATIONAL MONETARY FUND:
INTRODUCTORY COMMENTS

THE FIRST thing of importance to say about the Bretton Woods monetary proposal is that it was agreed to by the delegates of 44 nations. As a proposal for international collaboration, the plan reveals, I think, a statesmanlike attitude toward world problems. That the plan is *broadly international* in character makes a strong appeal, I believe, to the smaller countries. That there is agreement by the technical experts of both the great and the small nations must be regarded as significant. It is a fact that cannot easily be brushed aside by any responsible government. It is a good start in international co-operation.

Purposes

The second thing that needs to be said is that the *details* are not the most important part of the plan. What is really important is that the plan sets up an international institution—an institution at work on international collaboration; an institution continually on the job, dealing with current international monetary developments and balance of payment problems; an institution constantly providing means of adjustment through international action.

The purposes of the International Monetary Fund can be set forth in summary fashion as follows:

1. To provide the machinery for international consultation.
2. To fix, after consultation with each member country, the postwar structure of exchange rates.
3. To promote exchange stability and to avoid competitive exchange depreciation.
4. To provide machinery for an orderly adjustment of exchange rates when needed to correct a fundamental disequilibrium.
5. To aid member countries to achieve balanced trade without resort to deflationary policies.
6. To assist in the removal as rapidly as possible of foreign-exchange restrictions that hamper world trade.

The Fund can help member countries to reach an international balance without forcing upon any country a policy of deflation. It is obvious that a country could easily reach a balance in its international account by undertaking a rigorous deflation of income and employment to a point where imports would be sharply curtailed. But such action does not promote world prosperity and world trade. It is the intent of the Fund to help countries reach a balance at a high level of production, employment and international trade. The use of the Fund's resources affords time for adjustment. It may be that an orderly adjustment of the exchange rate is required. It may be that the country that is out of balance should undertake a program of development and diversification of its industries and agriculture. Such a development program (aided, perhaps, by the Bank for Reconstruction and Development) may make certain imports unnecessary and may create export possibilities. Thus a new balance could be reached. Temporary borrowing at the Fund to meet its current payments may enable a country to make such adjustment without in the meantime being forced to take uneconomic measures destructive of world prosperity and world trade.

The Bretton Woods proposal seeks to promote stability of

exchange rates without running the risks involved in a rigid fixity of rates. This is the crux of the matter. The serious defect in the old rigid gold standard was that it compelled a country to adjust its entire structure of prices, wages and incomes to the fixed exchange rate. On the face of it, it is no exaggeration to say that this was an absurd procedure. It amounted to demanding that the whole vast internal economic structure be continually compelled to revolve around the pivot of the fixed exchange rate.

England's Experience under the Gold Standard

Consider the experience of England following the last war. It was a hotly debated question whether England should return to the old gold parity or adjust her foreign-exchange rate to the changed internal level of prices, wages and incomes. There was divided opinion. The economists and large sections of industry were in favor of adjusting the exchange rate to the internal structure. But the older financial point of view prevailed. England returned to the old gold parity.

What happened? The internal structure of prices, wages and incomes was gradually and progressively deflated. The process was a painful one. Prices declined, the burden of debt increased and there was widespread unemployment. The required adjustment creaked and groaned and never was completely made. In the end, England was driven off the gold standard.

In consequence of this painful experience, all sections of British public opinion underwent a widespread educational process. With negligible exceptions, the British public is through with the idea that the whole internal economy must revolve around a fixed exchange rate. They are now committed to the opposite program of adjusting the exchange rate to the requirements set by the internal level of prices, wages and incomes.

Orderly Adjustment

How to square the theory of exchange adjustment to reasonable stability of exchange rates—that is the problem that confronts the modern world. The proposed international monetary plan is an answer to this problem. Under the plan, no individual member country is allowed to engage in competitive exchange depreciation; instead, it is proposed that adjustment of exchange rates must be made through international collaboration. The provisions in the plan for exchange adjustment are as follows:

1. After consulting the Fund, a member country may change the parity of its currency (par value of all currencies is expressed in terms of gold) without approval of the Fund but not to exceed 10 per cent. Member countries agree, however, not to propose a change in the parity of their currency unless such change is necessary to correct disequilibrium. Competitive exchange depreciation is ruled out.

2. The plan requires that the Fund shall approve a requested change in the par value of a currency (in addition to the limited change referred to above) if essential to the correction of a fundamental disequilibrium. The Fund may not demand that a country must force its domestic price, wage and income structure into line with the existing exchange rate. In accordance with the British experience cited above, the Fund is asked to permit the exchange rate to be adjusted to the requirements of the internal price and income structure; not the other way around. The plan is designed to prevent a rigid exchange situation from forcing deflation upon the world. Approval by the Fund requires only a majority vote.

3. Should the Fund refuse an adjustment of the exchange rate needed to correct a fundamental disequilibrium, a member country may withdraw at a moment's notice. In the final analy-

sis, therefore, the Fund cannot coerce a country into a deflationary policy against its own wishes. This provision is of the utmost importance.

Transition Period

The plan specifically provides for the continuation of exchange control during the postwar transition period. This insures that the resources of the Fund will not quickly be exhausted in a premature effort to remove restrictions.

Exchange control should indeed, as the plan provides, be removed by progressive stages as soon as the underlying facts warrant. But in the chaotic conditions in which many countries will find themselves for many months and even years following the war, removal of these controls could be disastrous. The plan provides that if exchange control is still in force after three years in any country the Fund shall report on the restrictions still in force; and if the restrictions continue after five years, such country must consult with the Fund with respect to a program leading to their removal.

Unsound Capital Movements Controlled

The Fund's resources cannot be used to finance speculative capital movements. "Hot money" flight—so disturbing in the thirties—would be stopped. The Fund may require a member country to exercise control to prevent such use of its funds.

The Role of Gold

A question frequently asked about the proposed plan is: What is its relation to gold? Gold plays an important part in the plan; yet the plan is not a return to the old gold standard. The currency of each country under the plan is indeed expressed in terms of gold. This is precisely similar to the gold standard. But unlike the gold standard, the parity can be adjusted through international collaboration so as to correct a disequilibrium without forcing upon countries deflationary policies that are destructive of national or international prosperity.

It is this feature of flexible adjustment that differentiates the proposed plan from the old gold standard. It is this feature that has caused a critic to label the plan, "How to go swimming without getting wet." A more accurate label, however, would be, "How to go swimming without drowning." Under the old rigid gold standard, a considerable number of guests at the swimming party were periodically submerged, and in the catastrophic depression beginning in 1929 the whole party barely escaped disaster.

A part of the gold holdings of member countries must be subscribed to the Fund. Moreover, if a country wishes to purchase foreign exchange with its own gold holdings, it is expected to do so through the Fund when it can do so with equal advantage. In addition, when the gold and foreign-exchange holdings of a member exceed its quota in the Fund, such country in buying foreign exchange from the Fund is required to use its own resources of gold and foreign exchange to an equal extent. Finally, if the member's gold holdings increase in any one year, and if it has already borrowed from the Fund, it must repay the loan to the same extent as it adds to its holdings of gold and foreign exchange. Thus in various ways, gold held outside of the Fund may be drawn into the Fund.

It is, however, a fact that under the plan, there would remain very large gold holdings outside of the Fund. Thus, huge gold movements could occur, indicating a major disequilibrium, while at the same time the accounts of the Fund were quite neatly in balance. However, it can be expected that the Governing Board of the Fund would certainly regard itself remiss in its duty if it failed to take account of such gold movements and took no steps to correct the disequilibrium.

The Fund has the power to make an agreed uniform change all around in the par value of all member currencies, provided, however, that every member country having 10 per cent or more of the aggregate quotas approves. This means, in practice, that if the United States, the United Kingdom and Russia approve, the Fund can reduce all around the price of gold. Such all-around change in the price of gold would not affect exchange rates.

The Fund, therefore, has the power to face up squarely with the gold problem. This problem could certainly not be solved by the United States alone. It can only be dealt with effectively through international collaboration.

The Fund has the power to face up with the gold problem because (*a*) it provides international collaboration to promote equilibrium and thereby to stop one-way gold movements and (*b*) it has the power to curtail uneconomic gold production by reducing the price of gold.

Subscriptions to the Fund are made in gold and in "currency." The subscription of each member is equal to its quota. The combined quotas of all countries are $8.8 billion, of which the share of the United States is $2,750 million. Each country must subscribe 25 per cent of its quota in gold or 10 per cent of its gold holdings, whichever is smaller. The rest of the quota is subscribed in "currency," as explained in the following chapter.

CHAPTER VII

The Functions of the International Monetary Fund

THE INTERNATIONAL MONETARY FUND would perform three major functions because it provides for (*a*) short-term credit to countries to help them over temporary difficulties in their balance of payment position, (b) mechanisms of adjustment to improve the long-term balance of payment position of member countries and (c) continuous machinery for international consultation, and for research, surveys and reports dealing with current international problems.

Any one of these three functions of the Fund would justify its existence. Combining all three functions, each reinforces the other. The Fund can therefore play a very important role in achieving international monetary stability and an orderly development of international monetary relations.

1. The Fund as a Short-Term Credit Institution

Discussion about the Fund not infrequently proceeds on the erroneous assumption that it is intended to supply virtually all the foreign exchange that any country will use. Nothing could be further from the truth. All countries will have international monetary reserves of gold and foreign-exchange balances entirely outside of the Fund. Some will have large monetary reserves and some small, relative to their needs. Foreign-exchange dealings will take place in the ordinary, private, foreign-exchange channels precisely as would be the case were no Fund in existence at all. In the usual case the resources of the Fund would not be used.

It is of the utmost importance to emphasize the point that the Fund is not intended to provide foreign exchange for its members in the usual case. The resources of the Fund are intended to supplement the ordinary foreign-exchange resources of the members and to constitute a second line of defense in meeting temporary balance of payment difficulties. The Fund guarantees each member a line of credit which it can draw upon when necessary. In this respect it provides insurance against a breakdown of international monetary arrangements.

Let us consider precisely why the Fund can accurately be described as an institution that provides a line of credit for its members. In order to be entitled to a line of credit each member makes an initial contribution to the Fund in gold amounting to 25 per cent of its quota, or 10 per cent of its gold holdings, whichever is smaller. It is estimated that the total amount of gold that will thus be contributed by all the members will amount to about $1,650 million. Thus the Fund will hold at the outset a certain amount of gold which may be used to purchase foreign exchange in any member country, since gold is universally acceptable all around.

In addition, however, each member, in order to obtain the line of credit referred to, agrees to put up a certain amount of "currency" upon becoming a member of the Fund. This currency may be either in the form of a deposit account entered in its Central Bank to the credit of the Fund or it may simply be a noninterest-bearing obligation of the member government deposited with the Central Bank to the credit of the Fund. The amount so deposited (whether as a deposit account or as a noninterest-bearing obligation) must be equal to the quota assigned the member country in the Fund minus the gold contribution made. In the case of fairly large gold-holding countries the amount so deposited to the credit of the Fund would be 75 per cent of its quota, 25 per cent of the quota being paid in gold. In the case, however, of countries having small gold holdings, only 10 per cent of their gold holdings will be deposited with the Fund, while the remaining part of the quota would be deposited in the Central Bank as a deposit account or as a noninterest-bearing demand obligation of the government.

An illuminating way of describing the nature of the Fund was suggested in a seminar at Harvard University by Dr. Eugenio Gudin, Chief of the Economic and Financial Council in Brazil. He represented the members of the Fund as seated around an oblong table. Upon the middle of this table is placed a large bowl into which all the countries deposit their gold contributions. In addition, each member country places its own individual bowl on the table. Into its own bowl the country deposits its nongold contribution in the form of a Central Bank deposit or of a noninterest-bearing government obligation. In the technical language of the Bretton Woods draft it is said that the country deposits its "currency." For the sake of brevity we shall use this term. Let it be remembered that whenever the term *currency* is so used it means a deposit account in the Central Bank of the member, or the deposit of a non-interest-bearing government obligation, both entered to the credit of the Fund.

Now let us return to Dr. Gudin's illustration. Brazil, let us say, has contributed 25 per cent of her quota in gold to the central gold bowl. In addition, Brazil has deposited in her own bowl her own *currency* equal to 75 per cent of the quota.

Let us now assume that Brazil finds herself short of foreign exchange and wishes to take advantage of her line of credit with the Fund. Let us assume that she wishes to obtain United States dollar exchange. She goes to the Fund and asks to borrow United States dollars from the Fund. The Fund is able to supply the dollars because the United States has contributed dollar *currency* in its bowl to the credit of the Fund. In order to borrow, however, Brazil is compelled to advance additional collateral over and above the amount already deposited. In other words, to the extent that Brazil wishes to borrow dollars she must put, so to speak, additional Brazilian *currency* into her individual bowl to the credit of the Fund. If Brazil borrows dollars equal in value to one-fourth of her quota, she will have added a further 25 per cent of her quota to the *currency* held in the Brazilian bowl.

What is the purpose of all this? Clearly one purpose is to insure that Brazil has put up an adequate amount of collateral for any foreign exchange that she has borrowed from the Fund. How much is this collateral? What is the ratio of the collateral put up to the line of credit used? In the event that the additional *currency* deposited amounts to 25 per cent of her quota, the collateral will be five times the amount borrowed. This is true since Brazil will have deposited into the central gold bowl and into her own individual *currency* bowl 125 per cent of her quota, while she has thus far borrowed only up to 25 per cent of her quota. The ratio of security that Brazil has provided for her borrowing is thus 5 to 1. In other words, the Fund holds security back of the loan made to Brazil in the form of gold equal to 100 per cent of the loan made and, in addition, Brazilian *currency* equal to four times the amount of the loan.

Let us assume that Brazil continues to borrow in each succeeding year 25 per cent of her quota until her borrowings have exhausted her full line of credit. The full line of credit that any member country is entitled to, it must be remembered, is equal to the quota assigned to each country plus the gold contributed. A country may not draw in any one year an amount in excess of 25 per cent of the quota. Thus it would take Brazil five years to exhaust her line of credit.

When Brazil has used her full line of credit, how much collateral will the Fund hold as security for the loan extended? The collateral, when the full line of credit is exhausted, is equal to nearly twice the amount of the loan. This is true because by the time Brazil has exhausted her full line of credit she will have been compelled to deposit in her bowl to the credit of the Fund 200 per cent of her quota in the form of her own *currency*, and in addition the 25 per cent of gold placed in the central bowl. Thus the gold and Brazilian *currency* combined will at this point equal 225 per cent of her quota. On the other side, her borrowing amounts to 125 per cent of her quota. The security Brazil has placed to the credit of the Fund to protect the loan therefore is, when she has used her full line of credit, in the ratio of nearly 2 to 1.

Let us briefly go back over the operation in order to make

it crystal clear. Brazil, upon becoming a member of the Fund, has already deposited 25 per cent of her quota in gold in the central bowl and 75 per cent in Brazilian *currency* in her own bowl, all of which deposits now become the property of the Fund. After having made these deposits, Brazil is now a full-fledged member and entitled to a line of credit equal to her quota plus the gold contribution. In order to borrow, however, she must deposit *additional* Brazilian *currency* to the credit of the Fund equal to the amount of foreign exchange she wishes to borrow. Thus the additional deposit, over and above the initial deposit, always equals dollar for dollar the amount she has borrowed from the Fund.

It is further provided that the gold value of the Fund's assets must be maintained. If the currency of a country has depreciated, such country must make good to the Fund any loss that the Fund has sustained in the gold value of its currency held by the Fund.

It will be seen from this illustration that the Fund is conducting a prudent lending business. There is always adequate security back of every loan.

This is not all. The Fund conducts its lending business on the sound credit policy of charging interest rates for the loan. Since it is intended that the Fund shall merely supplement the ordinary foreign-exchange operations, members are expected to borrow only to meet temporary difficulties. They are not expected to exhaust their full line of credit or to continue the loan on a long-term basis.

In order to deter a country from using its line of credit in excess of the amount required to meet short-term emergencies, the rate charged rises the larger the amount that is borrowed. If a country used only one-fourth of its line of credit, the rate is moderate. If it has used its full amount, the charges rise to a substantially higher figure.

Moreover, if a country repays the loan in a short period of

time, the rate charged is low. If, however, a country allows the loan to run for several years, the interest rate rises progressively the longer the duration of the loan. Thus the rate rises in two dimensions: (*a*) the larger the amount of the loan and (*b*) the longer the period for which the loan runs. And finally, if the combined effect of the size of the loan and the period of the loan is such as to reach the rate of 4 per cent, the Fund and the members are to consider means by which the loan may be reduced. If, however, the loan is continued and the charges rise to 5 per cent, the Fund may then raise the rate to any level deemed appropriate as a penalty for a country abusing its line of credit. The Fund is designed to provide short-term credit only. If a country abuses the privilege, it is appropriate that a heavy penalty charge be applied.

2. The Fund as an Institution to Insure Orderly Adjustment of Exchange Rates

Let me repeat again that the resources of the Fund merely constitute a supplement to the ordinary, private, foreign-exchange operations. It is conceivable that the resources of the Fund may be used relatively seldom or only by a relatively small number of countries or at any rate by countries whose share in the total world trade is relatively small. In fact it is, I think, likely that the Fund will be used a good deal, although *relatively* seldom compared with the volume of private foreign-exchange transactions conducted outside of the Fund. Should it, however, prove true that no member used its line of credit with the Fund at all, it would by no means follow that the Fund would not perform a useful purpose. The line of credit, though unused, would have the great value of providing confidence and security to countries. Thus protected they would be in a position to go forward without imposing unnecessary restrictive measures to safeguard their balance of payment position—measures that could only operate to curtail the volume of world trade and thus injure the whole world economy.

Quite apart from the line of credit afforded by the Fund and quite apart from the extent to which it is used or merely held in reserve, there are other functions which by themselves alone justify the establishment of the Fund. Countries do feel, in fact, the need of a line of credit to help them over their short-run balance of payment problems. But even though this were not the case, an international monetary agency with authority to regularize orderly changes in exchange rates would still be needed. If there were no such international agency, countries would be quite free to engage in irresponsible and competitive currency depreciation.

It is well known that no one can say now what the proper foreign-exchange value of the currencies of most countries in the world should be in the postwar period. We shall have to find by experimentation and experience what the appropriate rate is. If every country were left free to make this decision quite on its own without international consultation, we can be sure that the process of experimentation and adjustment would be a very chaotic and disturbing one. No country can be sufficiently objective to set an exchange rate that will not tend to give it an undue advantage. When every country seeks to attain an unduly favorable exchange rate, the whole world is let loose upon a stormy sea of competitive exchange depreciation.

The Fund provides machinery for a careful determination of the initial exchange rate and for an orderly process of adjustment in the difficult transition period. It provides for consultation, study and joint determination of the exchange rates between the member country in question and the authorities of the Fund. Such a procedure will permit the finding of a proper exchange rate during the period of trial and error and of experimentation.

The orderly determination of an appropriate exchange rate

is one of the urgent problems that must be dealt with in the transition period. This is one of the reasons why it is important that the Fund be soon established. If the Fund is not established at an early date, there would be no international agency to assist in an orderly and objective manner in finding appropriate exchange rates in the transition period from war to peace.

Also, for the long run it is equally important that an international agency be established to provide for orderly changes of exchange rates whenever economic developments indicate that such changes would be desirable from the standpoint of international monetary stability.

Those who argue that there is no need for such an international agency, that all we need to do is to re-establish the old rigid gold standard, are fighting for a lost cause. The old gold standard cannot be reconstituted. There is not one of the group of democratic nations of northern or western Europe that would join in the re-establishment of the gold standard. The reasons for this have already been explained in the preceding chapter. No country will again sacrifice the goal of internal stability and full employment on the altar of the gold standard. To repeat, they will not permit their internal structure of income, wages and prices to be deflated to meet the requirements of a rigid foreign-exchange rate. On the contrary, they insist, and rightly so, that the first consideration must be internal economic stability and full employment and that the foreign-exchange rates must be adjusted so as to promote and sustain these domestic ends.

The orderly adjustment of exchange rates to the requirements of internal stability and full employment offers the means by which we can achieve at one and the same time both internal stability and full employment and, on the other hand, international stability and a high level of world trade. It is not difficult to see that a high level of world trade can only be achieved when the various countries have high levels of business activity and employment at home. It is also not difficult to see that the orderly adjustment of exchange rates promotes both internal and international stability. The orderly adjustment of exchange rates does not mean that one country undercuts another. On the contrary, it means an exchange rate that keeps every country in an appropriate balance with the rest of the world. An orderly adjustment of exchange rates means that no country will be permitted to take an unfair advantage of other countries in foreign-exchange markets. It means the fixing of exchange rates so that the various countries will be on a fair competitive basis one with the other. Since the artificial advantage of competitive currency depreciation will not be tolerated, each country must face the world market in terms of efficiency and productivity. Each country will be able to sell those products in which it has the highest economic efficiency in terms of human skills and natural resources.

3. The International Monetary Fund as a Means for International Consultation

The Fund will be concerned not merely with the immediate and specific problem of making appropriate orderly changes in the exchange rates. It will be concerned with far more fundamental problems of international co-operation and of promoting a balanced development of world trade and world production. One of the purposes of the Fund as set out in Article I is: "To facilitate the expansion and balanced growth of international trade, and to contribute thereby to the promotion and maintenance of high levels of employment and real income and to the development of the productive resources of all members as primary objectives of economic policy."

To this end the Fund is obligated to engage in continuous research on international conditions and developments with a view to discovering measures that will promote balance. The statutes of the Fund provide that if any member is using the resources of the Fund in a manner contrary to its purposes, the Fund shall make a report to the member, setting forth the factors involved that tend to upset the general world balance, and in particular the lack of balance between the member in question and the rest of the world. It is further provided in the statutes that the Fund may by a two-thirds majority vote publish a report to any member regarding any monetary or economic conditions and developments in such member country that directly tend to produce a serious international disequilibrium. The Fund may, moreover, communicate at any time information to any member regarding such matters.

An international agency armed with powers to obtain adequate information from the various member countries and entrusted with the duty of analyzing and reporting to the entire world on this information will contribute very greatly to an orderly world development. It was generally recognized, for example, that one of the important contributing factors to the chaotic development in the late twenties and early thirties was complete lack of information about short-term international balances held abroad by each of the leading creditor countries. If it had been known how fantastically large these short-term holdings then were, we can be sure that financial institutions, both public and private, would have managed their affairs in a more prudent manner.

The statutes of the Fund require each member to furnish information deemed necessary to promote the functions and purposes of the Fund and to enable it to discharge effectively its duties. The information that may be requested involves data, among other things, on the following items:

1. Official and private holdings at home and abroad of gold and foreign exchange.
2. International balance of payments of each country.

3. International investment position of each country.
4. National income of member countries.
5. Commodity price indices.
6. Comprehensive statement of exchange controls, if any are in effect in the various countries.
7. Amounts awaiting clearance in commercial and financial transactions where official clearing arrangements exist and the length of time during which such arrangements have been outstanding.

The Fund will accordingly enlarge the fund of information upon which each country can plan an orderly program of adjustment of its economic life in relation to the world economy. This function alone would justify the establishment of the International Monetary Fund.

Conclusions with Respect to the Functions of the Fund

To repeat, any one of the three functions discussed above would justify the establishment of the Fund. Taking them all together each function reinforces the other. The function of gathering information, of engaging in research, of making reports with respect to economic conditions and developments throughout the world, of communicating views to member countries with respect to its own internal economic conditions and development in relation to the international situation—all of this will help to maintain a world balance. In so far as this is the case, the performance of this function would of itself minimize the extent to which orderly adjustment of exchange rates may become necessary and the extent to which any member needs to draw upon its line of credit with the Fund. Indeed, it would be a most happy situation if these latter functions should not need to be performed at all. So smooth and happy a development is not at all humanly probable. It will doubtless become necessary to make from time to time an orderly adjustment in exchange rates; and it will become necessary for the member countries from time to time to draw upon their line of credit with the Fund.

CHAPTER VIII

CRITICISMS OF THE INTERNATIONAL MONETARY FUND

MANY criticisms have been directed against the International Monetary Fund. This is not to be wondered at. Every new institution has to run the gauntlet of criticism. And this is as it should be. If an institution cannot stand up against criticism, there is probably something wrong with it. We must be sure that there is a genuine need for a Monetary Fund and that it will accomplish reasonably well the ends sought.

Fund Is Too Large

One criticism is that the Fund is grandiose and overly ambitious; that it is too large. It is argued that many countries have large reserves of gold and dollars. Some have even asserted that there is no need for any Fund to supplement the existing holdings of international monetary reserves.[1]

It is true that many countries have substantial international monetary reserves. But unfortunately this is far from true of all countries. Thus China, Czechoslovakia, Poland and Greece, for example, have quite inadequate international monetary re-

[1] For a succinct discussion of the criticisms of the Fund, *see* my essay in *International Financial Stabilization, a Symposium*, published by the Irving Trust Company, New York, December, 1944.

serves, and many other countries which hold only moderate reserves need a line of credit to fall back upon. There is therefore a genuine need for a Fund.

If a Fund is to be set up it is not difficult for anyone who has even a little knowledge of the difficulties of international agreement to see that the quotas assigned to different countries must have some reasonable relation to the economic position of each country in the world economy regardless of the current distribution of international monetary reserves. It is not possible to set up a Fund that supplies foreign exchange for the needy countries without providing a contingent supply for those less needy. Such a program might, indeed, be ethically and morally desirable, but it is not practical international politics. If some countries are given access to the Fund, all member countries must be given substantially equal privileges commensurate with their position in the world economy. They may currently not need to use the Fund, but the time may come when they will.

Moreover, it is difficult to see what harm is done by allowing all countries a limited and controlled line of credit in relation to an agreed-upon quota for each country. If the country does not need the line of credit, it may never be used. But it is there as protection and insurance, and in this respect can only do good.

With respect to the size of the Fund, it must be remembered that in the nature of the case not all members can be borrowers at the same time. By and large, if half are borrowers, the other half are lenders. Thus, as a rough first approximation, we should think of the resources of the Fund as $4.4 billion not $8.8 billion.

Sterling-Blocked Balances

No monetary arrangement, it is said, can have any validity until this problem is squarely faced. The Fund side-steps it. The delegates were generally agreed that this problem could not and should not be saddled on the Fund. The Fund could not perform its functions, having to do with current transactions, if it undertook to assume responsibility for international indebtedness arising out of the war. Such an undertaking would wreck the Fund. The problem of war indebtedness must be taken care of by other means—by lend-lease arrangements, by long-term financing and by special arrangements between Britain and her creditors. If, indeed, an international institution were needed, it should certainly not be the Fund, which has quite other functions to perform.

Abuse of Fund

Some critics have argued that countries with adequate international monetary reserves outside of the Fund may abuse the privilege of the Fund by safeguarding their own reserves and using their line of credit with the Fund. This criticism is based on a misunderstanding of the provisions. It is not possible for a member that has large international monetary reserves outside of the Fund to abuse its line of credit with the Fund. There is a provision that if a member country has reserves outside of the Fund in excess of its quota, it must keep a reasonable balance between the use of its own reserves and the use made of the resources of the Fund. It is provided that such member must use its own resources, as a minimum, at a rate equal to its use of the Fund. And if its own monetary reserves increase, it must reduce its past borrowings at the Fund at a rate equal to the increase in its outside monetary holdings. Other possible abuses are discussed below in connection with other problems.

Fund Promises Too Much

Another criticism is that the Fund promises more than it can live up to. The Fund Agreement provides that member nations shall be entitled to obtain under the conditions stated up to a total of $8.8 billion worth of foreign exchange.

The first reply to this criticism is that the countries cannot all be debtors at the same time. If some are debtors, others are creditors.

If, however, the demands upon the Fund for foreign exchange were concentrated exclusively upon dollars, the total demand would be the combined quotas of all foreign countries, ($6,050 million) plus their gold contributions, or a total of about $7 billion. The Fund, however, does not have that amount of dollars to sell. The dollars available in the Fund would in the first instance amount to the $2,750 million contributed by the United States plus the gold contributions of all the other countries amounting to around $1 billion. Thus the possible demand for dollars in the Fund would be around $7 billion while the total supply of dollars in the Fund is slightly under $4 billion. There is, therefore, a gap between the possible demand for dollars and the available supply of dollars in the Fund, and some critics have urged that this gap presents a serious dilemma for which the Fund Agreement offers no solution.

If, indeed, the Fund Agreement took no account of the problem, something evidently was overlooked by the experts. The fact is, however, that the Conference was thoroughly conscious of the problem as is evident from various provisions contained in the Fund Agreement.

Before considering these provisions, however, let us consider the probability that a dollar shortage in the Fund is likely to occur. I do not believe that there is any strong probability that this is likely to happen. In the first place, as we have already seen, the amount of gold and dollar balances held by foreign countries outside of the Fund is large. The Fund, as we have already explained, is not regarded as a main source of supply of foreign exchange. It is merely supplemental to the regular private-exchange operations. In the usual case, countries will regard their line of credit with the Fund as a last resort and will husband this line of credit carefully. The Fund Agreement provides that member countries may within a period of 12 months borrow no more than 25 per cent of their quotas. In the early chaotic transition years the countries under the greatest pressure to import will continue to maintain exchange control. By this means they can and will restrict unnecessary imports and thereby hold in check any excessive demand for dollars. Thus the dollar supply at the disposal of the Fund is not likely to be rapidly exhausted.

It is, moreover, quite unreasonable to suppose that foreign countries will restrict their demand for exchange, in their dealings with the Fund, exclusively to United States dollars. There will certainly be a demand for other currencies as well, especially Canadian dollars. It is not easy to see beforehand in just what direction the demand for exchange will run. Admittedly, it is probable that the major demand may run toward the United States. Yet if the United States should engage in relatively large international loans, and if it maintains a high level of income and employment at home, the supply of dollars currently made available outside of the Fund may prove to be quite adequate. Thus the demand for dollars from the Fund may not prove to be unduly large.

Before dollars in the Fund could become scarce, disequilibrium in the United States' international account would have persisted on a stupendous scale over many years. Many countries hold large reserves of gold and dollar balances outside of the Fund and others hold moderate but still fairly large amounts. Some countries with adequate monetary reserves would probably not come to the Fund for dollars at all. Those that do would, under the provisions of the Fund, have to use their own monetary reserves at the same rate as they used the resources of the Fund. Members with monetary reserves above their quotas must reduce their borrowings at the Fund whenever their monetary reserves rise. Moreover, the repurchase clauses tend to conserve the resources of the Fund for countries most in need of currencies that are likely to become scarce. Thus, everything considered, before the $3.7 billion initially available in the Fund could be exhausted, the gap in the United States' balance of payments would have had to be enormously large. This would mean that no fundamental solution of the United States international position had been reached.

It would be the function of the Fund to remedy such disequilibrium, partly by necessary adjustment of exchange rates, partly by a process of consultation with member countries with respect to economic conditions and developments in the various countries, and partly by long-term international loans made or guaranteed by the International Bank for Reconstruction and Development. In short, before dollars could become scarce in the Fund, the member countries both individually and collectively would have demonstrated their utter incapacity to manage their economic affairs so as to achieve a reasonably moderate degree of internal and international stability. There is no good reason to take so pessimistic a view.

At long last, however, should it turn out that dollars available in the Fund do become scarce, the Fund Agreement makes provision for this eventuality. It is provided that any currency that becomes scarce shall be rationed among the member countries. Since there are not enough dollars to go around, the different countries will be allowed their fair share of dollars so as to bring the supply and demand into balance. Each country will be permitted to impose limitations on exchange operations in the scarce currency.

Let it be noted that the problem of a possible shortage of dollars is not one created by the Fund. Dollars are surely more likely to become scarce without a Fund than with a Fund. This is true on the one hand because the Fund adds to the supply of dollars and on the other because the Fund through orderly adjustment of exchange rates and measures for the balanced development of world trade will tend to prevent a shortage of dollars.

If no Fund were established, what would happen if dollars became scarce? Foreigners would restrict purchases from the United States. Or if exports from the United States continued, balances owing to American exporters would be piling up in various countries. They would be unable to get payment for their exports.

Those who feel strongly that the possible "dollar gap" in the Fund should be closed may urge that the contributions to the Fund be raised all around to about double the line of credit afforded each country. If the United States' contribution were raised to $6 billion, the gap would be closed. It is not probable, however, that so large a contribution would be acceptable politically. Nor is it reasonable to suppose that so large a contribution is necessary. In all financial undertakings some reasonable risk must be assumed. The ratio of two to one between maximum demand for dollars in the Fund and the supply of dollars is a reasonable risk to run, considering the monetary reserves held outside of the Fund and the powers of the Fund to achieve an international balance. Every commercial bank runs an analogous risk. Its demand liabilities greatly exceed its cash resources, yet we do not compel it to "close this gap" by requiring a 100 per cent reserve.

Should the Fund run out of dollars, this would not mean that dollars were necessarily scarce all around. Many countries not responsible for the dollar shortage in the Fund might hold large gold and dollar balances. Their imports from the United States need not be restricted. Thus the existence of the Fund could in no way intensify the problem of dollar shortage. On the contrary, in various ways, as indicated above, the Fund would diminish the problem.

If some countries hoard dollar balances, then dollar shortages may occur even though the United States' international account were in balance. This is true with or without a Fund. But this is not likely to prove serious in practice. Countries are not likely to hoard dollar balances in any volume since they will need these funds for imports either from the United States or from other countries. No general problem could arise unless dollar balances were hoarded or converted into gold. The Fund could in various ways help to restrain any such tendency if it assumed unreasonable proportions.

With respect to the problem of dollar balances accruing from trade with third countries, the Fund Agreement contains provisions for the recapture of any dollars thus acquired by any country that has previously borrowed from the Fund.

No Fund mechanism per se can solve the fundamental problem of the United States' balance of payments. To expect that would be to look for a magic wand. The repurchase and rationing provisions accomplish all that mere mechanics can do. The Fund can, however, contribute to the problem in a fundamental way by wise management looking toward collective and individual action by member countries to achieve a balanced condition in world trade.

Finally, we must not lose perspective. The world will not come to an end should the reserve ratios of the Federal Reserve Banks reach the legal limit; nor will it come to an end should the Fund run out of dollars. These criteria are signposts, but they are not ends in themselves. Let us not set up a new golden calf, whose worship might restrain us from our real goals, which are expansion, high employment and world-wide prosperity. Should the Fund run out of dollars, it may be hoped that we will not prove so bankrupt of ideas as to permit policies that would be destructive of national and international prosperity.

Quotas Unreasonable

Some critics have alleged that the quotas established in the Fund are not based on realistic considerations of credit needs or credit-worthiness. To be sure, the matter of fixing the quotas was an extremely difficult one. Yet, in fact, with a few exceptions the quotas assigned were accepted as reasonable and satisfactory by the delegates from the various countries. The quotas do correspond fairly well to the trade and economic position of each country in the world economy.

Credit needs and credit-worthiness are likely to be conflicting concepts and the very use of these terms indicates how difficult the problem of appropriate quota assignments is. A country with large credit needs may not be a country whose credit is strong and dependable.

That the credit needs have been reasonably well taken care of is indicated by the spirit of good will and enthusiastic cooperation with which the various delegates accepted, with minor qualifications, the quota arrangements.

The idea that a quota should be assigned on a strict basis of credit-worthiness is wholly untenable. This suggestion misses the whole spirit and purpose of the Fund. It is the deliberate intent of the Fund that the various member countries should form a credit pool in which all take a limited risk in the interest of the workability and functioning of the whole world economy. It is the underlying philosophy of the Fund that the assumption of such mutual risk is precisely the necessary basis for a high level of production and trade throughout the world.

The willingness of countries to enter into a mutual arrangement to promote the prosperity of all members augurs well for the future. It is precisely such action that tends to create a condition of credit-worthiness. To do nothing for any country until it has reached a position of credit-worthiness would be a policy of negation. The assumption of risk by leading countries as well as by private enterprise is essential if we are to have an expanding and prosperous world. The limited risk that each country undertakes will, I think, be regarded by reasonable persons as small in view of the probable gains that may be achieved.

The risk involved is, in fact, small. It cannot be seriously contended by even the most cautious person that the United States stands to lose the whole quota of $2,750 million that it contributes. There is probably no person so cynical and skeptical as to believe that Canada, England, France, Australia, Holland, Belgium and many other countries are going to become so bankrupt that their currencies and other collateral deposited with the Fund will become worthless. And even for the weaker countries it must be remembered that if their currency should depreciate they must make good the dollar value of their deposits with the Fund. Moreover, attention should again be called to the fact that each country that borrows from the Fund would as a very minimum always be required to deposit with the Fund an amount of its own currency or other collateral equal to nearly twice the amount of the loan. The Fund arrangement, in fact, is from a financial standpoint a conservative and cautious one.

Fund Really Amounts to International Pump-Priming

It has been said that the Fund is apparently based on the conception that foreign trade should be expanded on the basis of the granting of credits, that the Fund amounts to a worldwide extension of deficit spending and pump-priming. The fear has, moreover, been expressed that America would supply the bulk of the credits.

I do not know whether underlying this criticism is the belief that the granting of all credit is inherently bad. There are some who take this position. There are extremists who argue that there ought to be no lending, no debts, no credits, either domestic or international. Were this so, all lending institutions would have to be condemned. But this extreme view is probably not intended since some who have voiced the criticism cited are themselves engaged in banking and lending operations, both at home and abroad.

The argument therefore must of necessity come to grips with the problem of the prudent and proper use of credit. The provision of short-term credit to meet a temporary gap in the current international account is no new proposal. Such short-term credits have been advanced by private banks throughout the history of modern capitalism. Private short-term credits will doubtless continue to play a role in minimizing the need for gold movements.

While a country is struggling to overcome temporary difficulties, it is a matter of precaution and safety to provide through the Fund a limited amount of short-term credit. Such a program will reassure countries and aid them in refraining from undue restrictionist measures which may seriously reduce the volume of world trade and unfavorably affect all countries. Indeed, it is a major function of short-term credits throughout the business world to prevent painful and unnecessary measures such as bankruptcy, for example, and, instead, to provide constructive means of getting out of the difficulty—means that will promote not only survival but also expansion and prosperity. A prudent banker is not one who has only one solution for his clients' difficulties, namely, putting them through the wringer; he is rather one who has sufficient ingenuity and courage to find constructive solutions for temporary difficulties.

That the Fund cannot be used as a long-run means of financing imports is evident from various provisions in the statutes. No member can borrow up to more than 25 per cent of its quota in any 12 months. If the loan runs for any extended period, higher and higher charges are imposed, and finally penalty charges. If a member is using the Fund for long-run purposes, the Fund may refuse further access to its resources.

The Fund Does Not Really Stabilize

The point just discussed leads to a consideration of a related criticism of the Fund. It is said that the Fund is really not a stabilization measure but only one that grants credits, and most likely credits to those who do not deserve them. It is argued that the Fund does not compel each member to "put its house in order." It is argued that the granting of credits is likely to lull the borrowing countries into a quite unsound financial international position. It is argued that the borrower is not required to "live within his means."

To all this a partial reply is that the critic has greatly overstated his case. It is not true that the Fund is obliged to hand out credits right and left to all comers regardless of the economic conditions and developments in the various countries. In fact, no member has an *unrestricted right* to draw upon its line of credit. The Fund Agreement specifically provides that the Fund may limit the use of its resources by any member whenever it is of the opinion that any country is drawing upon the Fund in a manner contrary to the purposes of the Fund. Moreover, as we have already seen, any member that borrows from the Fund must pay higher and higher charges the larger the amount of borrowing and the longer the period of the borrowing. And finally, when the amount and the period combined reach a certain point the Fund may charge any rate deemed appropriate as a penalty for the misuse of the Fund. In addition, attention may again be called to the point that the Fund has the power to make reports to any member country regarding economic conditions and developments within that country which tend to produce a serious disequilibrium in its international account. It is therefore not true that member countries may act in an irresponsible manner with respect to their international economic conditions and developments and at the same time expect to get credits from the Fund.

The "putting its house in order" type of criticism is frequently stated specifically in the language of orthodox finance. It has been said by many critics that the Fund misses the whole point of monetary stabilization when it does not set forth as a first requirement of each member that it balance its budget. The Fund, indeed, places no such requirement upon its members. The clash between the supporters of the Fund and its critics with respect to this point is a most fundamental one. This controversy relates to the question: What is indeed a sound fiscal policy? The modern view is that it is the aim and goal of fiscal policy to promote economic stability, to prevent both inflationary and deflationary developments. If private expenditures run so high in an intense boom that the demand for goods and services is outrunning the available supply of goods and services, then it is sound fiscal policy to have an overbalanced budget, to impose taxes in excess of expeditures and to reduce the public debt. If, however, there is depression and the flow of private expenditures is so low that prices are falling and unemployment is rapidly rising, then it is sound fiscal policy to unbalance the budget, to increase the volume of useful and productive public expenditures in excess of the current volume of tax receipts.

Those who demand as an end and goal in itself a balanced budget cannot in the nature of the case at the same time adhere to the goal of economic stability. From the long-run standpoint it is indeed possible (though not necessarily the best policy) to adopt expenditures and tax measures that will permit a long-run balancing of the budget and at the same time achieve economic stability. But from the standpoint of the fluctuations of the cycle, it is not possible to do so. The supporters of the Fund believe that promotion of economic stability is of the utmost importance and they believe that a flexible fiscal policy is an appropriate and powerful means for promoting economic stability. The Fund does not, therefore, demand that each member balance its budget. Herein lies the nub of the controversy.

But in a deeper sense, the answer to the criticism listed above is that the Fund is founded in a spirit of mutual collaboration, consultation and good faith. This principle is utterly foreign to the psychology of those who demand that the Fund prescribe and dictate to each member. The Fund is not conceived in terms of a mid-nineteenth-century schoolmaster with whip in hand to discipline each pupil. In the modern world an international institution founded on the principle of discipline and coercion would have not the slightest chance of success. Those who argue in these terms have failed to grasp the temper of the world in which we live.

It is perfectly true that there are wide differences in the family of nations with respect to achieved standards of financial conduct. There are also enormous differences in the degree to which countries have "grown up" with respect to monetary and fiscal management. But they are all eager to learn and to improve. The leaders in many countries are indeed aware that their governments will, partly by reason of inexperience and ignorance, partly by reason of inadequate self-discipline among their peoples, make innumerable mistakes and commit many economic "sins." Perfection will not be achieved even by the best countries, and something far below perfection must be expected for a long time in many parts of the world. To say these things is merely to state the problems confronting the family of nations. They are not merely problems set by the economic conditions of our times. They are also problems of education and national character.

But the time is past when the strong nations can wield a stick over the weaker ones. International security and economic prosperity must be developed in terms of mutual co-operation and mutual good will. And there is no need for cynicism and despair. Those who in recent years have been in intimate touch with the leaders of the various countries great and small must be heartened to see the growing devotion to the common ends which all members of the family of nations must strive to achieve.

It cannot be emphasized too strongly that the Fund is founded in the spirit of consultation, collaboration and good will. If, in fact, it turns out that it cannot succeed on this basis, then success on any terms is not attainable. In international relations the good-neighbor policy which involves consultation and co-operation has definitely and irretrievably superseded the policy of dictation and coercion.

Not a Two-Way Adjustment Program

With respect to mutual give and take in the relation of members to each other, it has been argued that the whole burden of adjustment, when disequilibrium in the balance of payment position of countries occurs, is placed in the Fund plan upon the creditor countries. Since the United States is generally assumed to be on the credit side of the ledger, it is specifically argued that the United States is called upon to shoulder the load.

Under the old gold standard it was typically the debtor country that had to make the major adjustment. The adjustment was not made by any direct attack upon its balance of payment position such as direct control of imports. The adjustment came automatically through the monetary and credit restrictions imposed by the outflow of gold and the banking adjustments that necessarily followed therefrom. Such credit restrictions resulted in a curtailment of business activity and employment and caused a fall in the national income. The consequence of the fall in the national income was to reduce the demand for foreign goods and so to bring about a better balance in its international accounts.

On the side of the creditor country an automatic adjustment was also expected to occur under the operations of the gold standard. The creditor country receiving an inflow of gold was expected to experience an expansion of credit and business activity, production, income and employment. With a higher level of income it was expected that the demand for foreign goods would rise. Thus on its side a contribution was made by the creditor country to an international balance.

The problem of adjustment as envisaged by the Fund Agreement is certainly very different from that contemplated under the gold standard. Were it not different, it would not be acceptable to any international conference today. The economic goals sought by countries today are not those that were sought under the old gold standard. The old slogans were rigid exchange rates and balanced budgets. The slogans today are full employment, rising living standards and economic stability avoiding both inflation and deflation. The fundamental difference between the old gold standard and the Fund is precisely that the process of adjustment and the achievement of international balance shall not come through internal deflation, depression and unemployment.

The adjustments contemplated under the Fund can, nevertheless, be described as two-way adjustments. But with respect to the debtor countries, they are not the adjustments typically envisaged under the gold standard. We shall elaborate upon this in a later paragraph.

So far as the creditor country is concerned the appropriate adjustment is substantially the same as that envisaged under the gold standard. But we can no longer rely upon automatic forces to bring this about. In the typical case the creditor country should undertake an expansion of employment and income and thereby increase its demand for foreign goods. But such expansion should not be allowed to develop to the point of inflation as it might and, indeed, in certain circumstances, did under the automatic processes of the gold standard. Expansion in the creditor countries should be held at the point of substantial full employment so as to maintain internal stability. In the long run, international stability is not promoted by inflationary developments in the creditor countries even though momentarily such a development might help to correct the current balance of payment position. No firm foundation for international stability can be laid upon any basis except that of internal stability in the various countries.

With respect to the debtor countries, we can no longer tolerate a method of adjustment that calls for internal deflation and unemployment. While such a procedure does momentarily help to correct the gap in the balance of payment, from the long-run and broader point of view it produces curtailment of world trade and tends to spread the disease of deflation and unemployment throughout the world. This creates a lack of balance in the cost-price structure in each separate country. It does not contribute to a healthy condition or to an effective functioning of the world economy.

If the gap in the balance of payments of a certain country is adjudged temporary, the country should be aided over its difficulties by the granting of credits through the Fund. If it is of a more fundamental and long-run character, an orderly adjustment of the exchange rate may be in order. But this is not necessarily the proper remedy. It may well be that something far more fundamental is necessary, such as a change in the structure of the country's imports and exports. It may be that the development of an agricultural program, or basic internal improvement projects which would foster new industries, may so change the character and volume of the exports and imports that a balance in the country's international account could be achieved. Such measures to promote a balance by the debtor countries are constructive and lead to higher incomes and to a larger volume of balanced world trade. Under no circumstances should any debtor country be required to make its adjustment, as under the old gold standard, through the process of deflation and unemployment.

Should it turn out that it may take considerable time for the basic disequilibrium to be corrected it may well be that the Fund should permit the member country to institute, in this interim period, exchange control. It is far better to introduce exchange control, and thereby limit the volume of imports to the most necessary commodities, than to curtail imports in general by means of the process of deflation and depression.

Thus we conclude that under the Fund a two-way adjustment is, in fact, contemplated. The adjustment calls for action on the part of both the debtor country and the creditor country. What is true, however, is that the type of two-way adjustment envisaged under the gold standard is not contemplated in the Fund Agreement and, indeed, would not be in line with current political thinking and policies.

To sum up this discussion, the gist of the matter is as follows. The two-way adjustment contemplated in the Fund Agreement requires policies that at one and the same time promote international stability and full employment in both the creditor and the debtor countries. The adjustments contemplated must be of a character that at one and the same time promote both internal stability and international stability. The one must not be sacrificed to the other. Under the gold standard, internal stability was not infrequently sacrificed to the goal of international stability. Under the gold-standard adjustment the debtor country might be forced into a serious deflationary process while the creditor country might run into an inflationary development.

The "Key-Currency Approach"

The view has been supported by a considerable segment of American opinion that a better solution of the problem of monetary stability is the "key-countries approach." This analysis has been ably and forcefully stated by Dean John H. Williams in various articles and recently in his *Postwar Monetary Plans*.[2] It is argued that international payments are typically made in terms of sterling or dollars, that these are the key currencies in the world, and that monetary stability primarily means stability of the sterling-dollar rate. With respect to the United States there should never be any question of exchange fluctuation. Variation in the dollar foreign-exchange rate would have very serious international repercussions which, in turn, would react unfavorably upon the United States. While England needs more latitude, nevertheless she also has an obligation as a great trading center to maintain exchange stability. For smaller countries greater latitude may be permitted. Thus the smaller countries may be left a large amount of freedom to tie in with the dollar or with sterling on such terms as best suits their internal prosperity. According to this view, therefore, there is no need for an International Monetary Fund. What is needed is close collaboration between the key countries, mainly England and the United States, with a large measure of flexibility and freedom for other countries.

The plan suggested is, in some measure, similar to the condition that existed in the late thirties before World War II. The British and the American stabilization funds collaborated informally to secure substantial stability in the dollar-sterling exchange rate. There was a sterling area to which a considerable number of countries, including the Dominions and the

[2] John H. Williams, *Postwar Monetary Plans and Other Essays*, Knopf, New York, 1944.

Scandinavian countries and some Latin-American countries, adhered. There was in effect also a dollar area including various Latin-American countries and to a degree Canada. While this arrangement prior to World War II was far from satisfactory, it must be admitted that there were many non-monetary causes for the unfavorable conditions then prevailing. These, it is hoped, could be removed in the peace following this war.

Against the key-country approach it has been urged by Mr. Rasminsky, Head of the Foreign Exchange Control Board in Canada, that such an arrangement tends to promote economic regionalism and the splitting up of the world into economic blocs. "The creation of blocs of this sort has in the past involved discrimination in trade as well as in currency matters." [3] Moreover, many small countries are "key countries" with respect to important commodities in world trade. Professor Robertson has said that "in the present state of world opinion the worst way to offer Anglo-American leadership to the nations in any field is to seem to be imposing it on them. That leadership must develop within the framework of a United Nations —and ultimately of a still broader—system." [4]

Consultation on international monetary matters which is restricted to informal discussion between the key countries and to which the small nations are not invited is likely to give rise to all manner of fears, frequently quite unfounded, but nevertheless disturbing. In fact, it can scarcely be questioned that the rights and interests of small nations cannot be so well taken care of under the key-country arrangement as through open and continuous international consultation in the International Monetary Fund.

Back in 1941 I was myself urging joint action between the

[3] Louis Rasminsky, "International Credit and Currency Plans," *Foreign Affairs*, July, 1944.
[4] D. H. Robertson, "The Postwar Monetary Plans," *Economic Journal*, December, 1943.

United States and Britain on (*a*) a parallel program of economic expansion, (*b*) developmental loans to backward countries and (*c*) monetary and economic stability. I quickly learned that such a program limited to these two great powers would be resented by other countries. The conception had to be enlarged and broadened so as to include all countries, great and small alike, in an international institution.

There is, nevertheless, an important core of truth in the key-country approach. But this is in no way at variance with the arrangement provided in the International Monetary Fund. The fact is that the International Monetary Fund cannot succeed except on the basis of the closest collaboration of the key countries. The Bretton Woods Conference itself is a striking illustration of the manner in which the key countries can successfully collaborate within the framework of an international organization. Without the closest collaboration and consultation of the leading countries the Bretton Woods Agreements could never have been achieved. Nevertheless, time and again the fact that proposals urged by the key countries had to be acceptable to all countries served as a useful check. The presence of the small countries, I think it will be generally agreed, helped to insure that the Agreements reached would provide a workable international arrangement.

In the political world federation which we are in process of instituting to preserve the peace of the world the great powers must play the leading role. But it is generally agreed that there is danger in the great-power approach unless these powers operate within the framework of an international institution in which all countries great and small alike are represented. So also in the economic sphere. The operation of the International Monetary Fund will devolve basically and fundamentally on the key countries. These countries can, however, co-operate to promote international stability more successfully within the framework of an international institution in which all countries participate. Fears, rivalries, jealousies and imputations of sinister purposes tend to vanish when the key countries are compelled to work together within the pattern of an international organization. The effectiveness of key-country collaboration is in no way diminished thereby; indeed, only when such collaboration takes place within the framework of a genuine international arrangement can its dangers be avoided.

Other Measures Should Come First

Finally, it has been urged that we have not put first things first. It has been said that we should first obtain international agreement with respect to tariffs, import quotas and other trade control measures. Others have suggested that all the problems of the transition period should first be fully taken care of; indeed, no monetary arrangement should be attempted until we have securely made the transition to a peacetime economy.

Consider the latter criticism first. It is true that certain measures must be undertaken outside of the Monetary Fund to take care of the transition period. Indeed, important measures have already been taken. The United Nations Relief and Rehabilitation Administration has been set up and is currently functioning. Thus relief measures are no part of the functions of the Fund.[5] In addition, preliminary conferences have been held and others are under way relating to such important transitional problems as shipping, control of air routes, oil, rubber, international cartels, commodity agreements, transplanted populations, the control and disposition of German industry and many other problems. The Fund cannot and is not designed to deal with innumerable complicated transitional problems. But it can and should help in an orderly transition to peacetime conditions not only by guiding international monetary develop-

[5] This separation Dean Williams has repeatedly and rightly urged, and later revisions of the monetary drafts have recognized the validity of this position.

ment through the transition period but also by providing a framework for long-run monetary stability. The Fund, along with other measures, can help to meet the difficult problems of the transition. In particular, the consultative parts of the Agreement can serve, during the transition, a very important function.

With respect to the other point—that international agreements should first be reached on commercial policy—the answer is, it seems to me, pretty obvious. There is no good reason why we cannot simultaneously move forward as rapidly as possible on the monetary front and on the tariff and commercial-policy fronts as well. Former Secretary Hull has for ten years been engaged in a Herculean effort to promote nondiscriminatory trade practices and to reduce trade barriers by means of trade agreements. Commercial-policy discussions are currently in progress and as soon as feasible an international conference dealing with tariffs and commercial policy should certainly be called.

Experience shows, however, that these are extraordinarily difficult matters to deal with. Those who suggest that monetary matters should be laid aside until the tariff problem is satisfactorily solved are either naïve or deliberately planning to postpone all action. No reasonable person will deny that the problem of tariff and trade control will not early reach any satisfactory conclusion. In particular, Secretary Hull, who has manfully striven for ten years against terrific opposition for a program of tariff reform, may be entitled to conceal a smile when it is suggested that a removal of tariffs and trade impediments should everywhere be accomplished before we tackle other urgent problems.

What I have said above in no way implies that tariff reductions and trade restrictions are not important. But we shall get nowhere if we attack tariffs first and neglect all other problems in the meantime. Instead of being too concerned about priorities we need to push forward with various measures as rapidly as is feasible. There is no one thing that has to be done first. Indeed, there would be violent disagreement about which should come first. No good can come from quarreling about priorities. Monetary stability will promote trade and world prosperity. And similarly, tariff reform and the progressive removal of trade restrictions will contribute to monetary stability. Each program supports the other.

Concluding Remarks

If no international monetary arrangements are set up, friction growing out of nationalist policies will be intensified. If collaborative international institutions are established, nationalist policies will still in some measure be present, but they will be ameliorated and we hope gradually reduced. International collaboration can progressively move toward a more stable and better functioning world economy.

If the United States fails to enter the monetary proposal, it may be feared that it will also remain aloof from other international economic institutions. While one may have high confidence that the United States this time will enter into international political arrangements to help secure the peace of the world, it remains to be seen whether we have reached a sufficient degree of understanding of economic world problems to embark upon economic collaboration. Having become international on political lines, there is danger that we shall remain isolationist on economic lines.

If the United States stays aloof from international economic arrangements, such institutions may still be set up under British leadership, including not only the members of the British Commonwealth of Nations but also the nations that can readily be drawn into the sterling area. Should such a development occur, intensified nationalist economic tendencies in the United States may be expected.

A partial international monetary union under British leadership would provide multilateral clearing among its members. But such a British union would necessarily seek to bring its payments into balance vis-à-vis the United States. Multilateral trade between the members of the sterling-area union would grow at the expense of American trade. This, in turn, would provoke the United States to build up its own dollar area, using foreign lending as a potent means to bring this about. The dangers of friction between the British Empire and the United States in such a development are obvious. It is such far-reaching problems as these that the United States must face in developing a responsible program—one that takes a long-run view of the interests of this country in terms of world-wide political and economic security.

The Bretton Woods Plans are international in scope. As such they are superior to bilateral arrangements. In the absence of broad international collaboration, nationalist policies tending toward economic isolation are almost certain to prevail. Or if not isolation, economic rivalries between blocs formed under the leadership of great nations. If collaboration on broadly international lines is not instituted, economic nationalism and isolationism, rival economic blocs and international friction will likely be intensified.

These proposals may be regarded as a test case. If the United States fails to accept these arrangements (in many respects less controversial and involving relatively small financial commitments) there is little probability that it will adhere to other needed international economic institutions. Yet if international economic institutions are not adhered to by the United States, can international political arrangements designed to secure the peace of the world succeed?

CHAPTER IX

INTERNATIONAL TRADE AUTHORITY

THE experience in the interwar period makes it quite clear that traditional approaches to the problem of trade and commercial policies are sterile and ineffective. It does no good merely to hold an international conference and make pious recommendations with respect to the removal of tariffs and trade restrictions. The experience in the interwar period shows that such recommendations produce no results. Worse yet, the more the experts recommended trade reductions, the more it seemed that those in charge of practical policy in the various countries resorted to increasing trade restrictions. We must make a fresh start on this problem.

Expansionist international trade policies cannot and will not be adopted and put into effect unless they constitute part and parcel of a broader program of international co-operation. If we begin with another international conference to reduce tariffs we shall again fail. But expansionist trade policies can become a part of a realistic program if incorporated in a wide framework of international economic collaboration.

Let me emphasize once again that no good comes from quarreling about what part of a broad international program must come first. Each reinforces and sustains the other, and each is necessary to the whole. In the nature of the case the whole integrated program cannot be adopted in a single conference. To attempt to do so would get us nowhere. It was right that at the Bretton Woods Conference attention was concentrated on monetary matters and foreign loans. But it was also essential that those who were laying monetary and financial plans should keep in mind the relation of these to other necessary parts of an international program. In making monetary and international investment plans it was important to have in mind in a general way the kind of trade policies which were deemed desirable and which monetary and investment policies could help to make realistic and workable.

We have learned that the removal of trade obstacles undertaken by itself alone is not a feasible program. A liberal trade policy must be undertaken side by side with a program of development, expansion and full employment throughout the world. Apart from these it can achieve nothing. Expansionist trade policies cannot and will not be adopted when every country is struggling for the largest possible share in a restricted domestic and international market. We must enlarge both the domestic and the international market—the domestic market by a policy of full employment at home, and the international by a policy of development in the industrially backward countries.

This is the lesson we have learned in the interwar period. It is for this reason that we have resolved this time not to neglect a program of development in the industrially backward countries. It is for this reason that the Bretton Woods Monetary and Financial Conference proposed the setting up of an International Bank for Reconstruction and Development. And it is for this reason that those concerned with international trade in the postwar period urge a domestic program of full employment, particularly in the great industrial countries. This is a new approach. Formerly, it was thought sufficient merely to urge the reduction of tariffs and the removal of trade barriers.

On the other side it would be a fatal mistake to become so enamored of international development and domestic full-employment programs that we forget all about international trade and commercial policy. International development and domestic full employment are not enough. We live in a world in which intercommunication and speedy transportation make self-sufficiency and economic isolation utterly impossible. It is not a question of trade or no trade. It is a question of the kind of trade relations we shall adopt. If we are to undertake international economic co-operation on expansionist and developmental lines it is evident that trade and commercial policy must become of paramount importance. We cannot escape this issue.

Development and expansion cannot succeed unless undertaken in a world which also plans appropriate international trade and commercial relations. For example, there would be no prospect that international loans could gradually be amortized and reasonable interest paid unless a high level of world trade were developed. Nor is there any prospect that the full benefits of a program of industrialization and development in the backward countries could lead to the desired levels of real income and living standards unless the countries whose productivity has been increased are able to trade on advantageous and nondiscriminatory terms throughout the world.

The notion that industrialization and development of the backward countries would result in a reduction of world trade is completely mistaken. All past experience shows that it is the highly productive countries with high purchasing power that constitute a large market for foreign products, and which, in turn, sell to other countries specialized products in which their resources and skills excel. The higher the productivity, the standards of living and the purchasing power of the now retarded countries, the larger will be their trade with the United States and with other highly developed countries.

In the final Act of the Bretton Woods Conference it was declared that the expansion and balanced growth of international trade could not be achieved through monetary and financial plans alone. The Conference therefore recommended that the participating governments, in addition to implementing the specific monetary and financial measures which were the main subject of the Conference, should create the necessary conditions in the field of international trade relations for the attainment of the broad goals the Conference had set out to achieve. It was recommended that the participating governments undertake ways and means of promoting mutually advantageous international commercial relations.

To achieve this end it is not sufficient merely to hold occasional international conferences on commercial policy. Continuous international collaboration on trade matters has in the modern world become imperative. It is therefore necessary, I believe, to establish a continuing organization—an International Trade Authority—which will always be on the job to promote the freest possible development of world trade.[1]

An International Trade Authority should be established before the end of the war alongside of the other international institutions that have already been proposed. Such an Authority should comprise all of the United Nations. It is evident that here, as also in the case of the Monetary Fund and the Bank for Reconstruction and Development, the great nations are bound to play the major role. But they should play this role within the framework of a United Nations organization. Only in this way can it be insured that the policies adopted genuinely promote not only the interests of the great nations but also those of the smaller countries. International good will and the good-neighbor policy require the formation of an all-inclusive international organization.

It would be the function of the International Trade Authority to promote the adoption of liberal and nondiscriminatory trade practices between the member countries. During the transition period immediately after the war it would be a part

[1] See P. W. Bidwell, "Controlling Trade after the War," *Foreign Affairs*, January, 1943.

of the task of the Authority, in co-operation with other international bodies, to direct the flow of trade so as to serve effectively the needs of relief and reconstruction. Afterward the Authority's main function would be to undertake a comprehensive study of long-range programs looking toward trade policies that would contribute to general world prosperity, a high level of international trade and the successful functioning of the various international agencies operating in their specialized fields.

The Authority should collect up-to-date information about trade policies currently in force in the different nations. It should study and report on the effect of such policies upon the world economy.

The member countries joining the Authority should agree to report any prospective changes in import or export duties or other trade practices, such as import or export licensing, import or export quotas, before putting any of these measures into effect. The member countries should agree that the proposed changes should not be put into operation within a reasonable period during which the Authority would have an opportunity to investigate the proposals. The Authority should study the proposals from the point of view whether the suggested changes in trade policy would threaten to disrupt international trade or have important adverse economic effects upon other countries and upon world prosperity in general. The Authority should be empowered to collect full evidence relating to such proposed changes and to make a report of its findings. This report should go to the country proposing the changes and should make a recommendation with respect to modification or abandonment.

It is not proposed that the member countries should turn over to the International Trade Authority the power to prescribe the trade or commercial policies of the member countries. Such action would involve a surrender of sovereignty which the nations of the world are today clearly unwilling to undertake. It is recommended, however, that the Authority be given the power to make an investigation and to report its findings and recommendations before the country is free to introduce the changes proposed. In this manner the pressure of world opinion can be brought to bear upon any individual country, strengthening the groups within the country that take an international point of view as opposed to a narrow nationalist policy which would be shortsighted. It could be a very great gain to provide through the investigation and recommendations of the Authority an over-all analysis designed to reveal the international implications of any proposed changes. In this manner the goal of genuine international economic co-operation could be furthered. It will not be possible to achieve a successful program of international economic collaboration unless the action of individual countries is continuously studied and viewed from the international angle. The reports and recommendations of the Authority would make it clear that a country cannot at one and the same time hope to obtain the benefits accruing from international economic collaboration while pursuing nationalist policies that defeat these ends.

If countries are to be persuaded, however, from undertaking nationalist policies, it is evident that the program of international collaboration must be positive and constructive. International economic co-operation cannot win support if we are always merely saying no, no. We can hope to persuade countries to desist from uneconomic international policies only in the event that we can point to a forward-looking expansionist and developmental program through international economic collaboration.

In undertaking a positive program of international economic collaboration it is urgently necessary for the International Trade Authority not to take a doctrinaire or dogmatic attitude.

It must not permit itself to become legalistic. It must not set up rules which in their specific application may at times defeat the broad purposes in view.

It is clear that a primary aim and goal of international trade policy should be to eliminate discriminatory practices. In earlier periods, when individual private trading was the universal rule and when tariffs constituted almost the only trade restrictions, the most-favored-nation rule served reasonably well as a means of eliminating discriminatory trade practices. It must be recognized, however, that trading methods have become enormously more diverse, complex and complicated than was formerly the case. Today there are countries that have a state trading monopoly, such as Russia, and there are other countries such as New Zealand where there is large state intervention involving bulk trades and other measures of state control. Some countries may find it desirable as a means of financing internal-development programs to classify imports from the standpoint of the degree to which they are essential to the economy, thereby enabling them to use their foreign-exchange resources for their more important needs. For some countries regional arrangements may be made involving a "customs union" with respect to certain commodities, while at the same time there may be national tariffs on other commodities. And some countries (the Danubian area, for example) may find that their productivity and real income would be promoted by regional preferential tariff arrangements.

In the complexity of modern trade conditions it is not possible to lay down any dogmatic rule that will serve the broad purpose of nondiscriminatory practice and general world-trade expansion. We shall not in the postwar period be living in any such simplified trading world as that of the nineteenth century. We shall be confronted with a great variety of trade practices. The International Trade Authority will have to keep firmly in mind the broad goals of nondiscrimination and trade expansion, but in so doing it must avoid the application of rigid doctrinaire rules.

It has never been a violation of most-favored-nation treatment for countries to form a complete customs union. It has, however, been regarded as inadmissible to make preferential tariff agreements that went halfway toward establishing a customs union—in other words lowering tariffs between the countries in question without raising them to other countries. Regional arrangements that reduce tariffs and trade restrictions and that treat other countries on a nondiscriminatory basis ought to be considered on their merits without being arbitrarily ruled out by application of rigid rules. If trade is promoted and countries outside of the regional arrangement are permitted to join if they so desire, such arrangements may deserve support no less than complete customs unions.

The fact that trade conditions in the postwar period will be characterized more than in the past by government trading, bulk purchasing, by regional arrangements that promote development and diversification in certain areas, and by developmental tariffs in backward countries, calls all the more for an International Trade Authority that would always be available to examine the merits and the practical operation of these complicated arrangements. The diversity of practice that we are likely to witness in the postwar period unless guided and controlled so as to promote and facilitate international economic co-operation is likely to be disruptive of world trade and to result in gross discrimination between countries.

Adjustments to changed conditions, if haphazard, may develop an immense amount of ill will and suspicion in international relations. To avoid these effects it will be necessary to guide the adjustments by consultation and agreement between nations. An International Trade Authority could here serve a useful purpose. It could become the meeting ground in which the member countries were able to lay their special problems before an impartial body which, viewing the whole from the international standpoint, could guide action in a manner that would broadly meet the needs of individual countries, yet in a manner designed to safeguard the interests of other countries, and, in general, promote equilibrium and world trade. The rule of reason would need to be applied instead of arbitrary and rigid rules. But nationalist policies disruptive of international collaboration should be strongly resisted. The Authority should grant or decline applications for special arrangements according to whether such arrangements could or could not be fitted into the general aims and goals of international economic collaboration. Such arrangements should always be viewed with respect to their effect upon world development and expansion and upon the general volume of world trade.

The Authority would be expected to prepare a code of fair-trade practices for international trade to be submitted to the member nations for adoption. Such a code once adopted could be administered by the Authority with appeals from its decisions to the International Court of Justice.

The International Trade Authority would be expected to work closely with other international organizations such as the International Monetary Fund, the International Bank for Reconstruction and Development, the Food and Agriculture Organization, the International Commodity Corporation, if established, and other similar agencies dealing with international economic policies. Through such co-operation the International Trade Authority could make an important contribution toward bringing about a more effective use of world resources, promoting an optimum international division of labor based upon the utmost development of resources both human and material throughout the world.

An International Trade Authority, and indeed other international economic agencies, could not function successfully unless an international security organization along political lines were established to promote continued world peace. Only on this basis could commercial policy be directed toward economic ends rather than toward ends designed to safeguard national defense in a world fearful of war. Genuine international economic collaboration involving a large measure of economic interdependence requires a peaceful world.

The Joint Declaration of President Roosevelt and Prime Minister Churchill, known as the Atlantic Charter, set forth as one of the common principles in the national policies of their respective countries the proposition that all countries, great and small alike, should have access on equal terms to the trade and to the raw materials of the world needed for their economic prosperity. It is evident that the implementation of such a declaration in actual practice confronts deeply ingrained and established policies all over the world which make it impossible to carry it out to a 100 per cent ideal degree. It is a broad aim toward which the world is working, but as is true of many aims it cannot all at once be achieved. Indeed, the Declaration itself introduced the qualifying phrase "with due respect for their existing obligations." Progress toward this high ideal would be furthered by an International Trade Authority constantly reviewing changes in the practices of member nations and examining the effect of such proposed changes upon the workability of the world economy.

In the Lend-Lease Agreements made between the United States, Great Britain and other United Nations, Article 7 makes the declaration that the terms and conditions under which benefits shall be provided to the United States in return for aid furnished shall be such as not to burden commerce between countries concerned. It is declared that the terms and conditions shall be such as to promote mutually advantageous economic relations between them and the betterment of worldwide economic relations in general. It is agreed that united action, open to participation by all other countries of like mind, shall be undertaken involving appropriate international and domestic measures directed to the expansion of production and employment and the exchange of goods which are the material foundations of the liberty and welfare of all peoples. It was agreed that the terms and conditions should be such as to eliminate all forms of discriminatory treatment in international commerce and to promote reduction of tariffs and other trade barriers.

The real answer to restrictionist trade practices must be found in an expansion of production and employment all over the world. In this the United States can play a leading role. First and foremost it must promote domestic full employment. Under conditions of full employment the United States will be a heavy importer of raw materials and unprocessed foodstuffs, of tourist travel services abroad, of luxury products of all kinds, and of many specialized articles that can to advantage be imported from other countries. For this reason the United States has a major interest in reducing restrictive international practices to a minimum and in favoring a progressive liberalization of commercial policy. The United States, having broken through the narrow confines of political isolationism with its concept of continental outposts within which self-defense is sought against a world in which we play no part, and having undertaken to play its role in establishing world-wide political security and world-wide conditions conducive to the preservation of peace, must as a corollary open up the freest possible world trade and intercommunication between all countries.

CHAPTER X

The United Nations Relief and Rehabilitation Administration

THIS agency, so essential for dealing with the problems of the transition period, is the outcome of a conference of representatives of 44 United Nations held in Atlantic City in December, 1943. It is designed to fill the urgent needs of relief and rehabilitation of the war-devastated countries as more and more areas become liberated.

It is expected that funds amounting to perhaps $2,500 million will be raised to pay for the supplies and services needed. It was suggested that each member country whose home territory has not been occupied by the enemy should contribute an amount approximately equal to 1 per cent of the income of the country for the year ending June 30, 1943. Accordingly, the contribution of the United States is $1,356 million, and that of the British Commonwealth nearly $500 million.[1]

It is not intended that the $2.5 billion, or whatever is subscribed, shall do the entire job. This sum will be supplemented by contributions from occupied countries and from private sources. No country desires free aid if it can be avoided. Most governments will pay for much of the goods and services received.

Following World War I various relief organizations were

[1] Cf. *UNRRA: Gateway to Recovery*, Nos. 30–31, National Planning Association.

established including an American Relief Administration. This
time it has wisely been decided to organize relief under the
banner of all the United Nations. This action represents the
new spirit of broadly international co-operation between great
and small countries alike. While it is clear that the United States
and the British Commonwealth of Nations must bear the overwhelming part of the burden, nevertheless, operating within
the pattern of an international agency to which the smaller
countries contribute according to their ability and capacity,
the cause of world unity and international good will is better
assured. Relief and rehabilitation are a matter of justice, not
charity. They should not assume the form of a charitable gift
by rich countries to those less fortunate.

The fact that every institution thus far set up or contemplated includes all the United Nations, large and small alike,
represents a major advance. The time is past when the great
nations can run the world alone.

"Relief and Rehabilitation"—these words indicate that the
functions of UNRRA are limited in scope. It is not intended
that this agency should undertake long-range programs of reconstruction. That is left for other agencies such as the Bank
for Reconstruction and Development. It is intended that
UNRRA will fill only the temporarily urgent needs.

Relief alone is clearly not adequate. It is not enough simply
to send in food, clothing and medicines to those in desperate
need. It is also necessary to revive the productive process; to
put the various nations back on their own feet; to provide seeds,
breeding animals, fertilizer, and essential repairs and parts for
machines. It is necessary to start these people on the road to
self-support.

Food

The first task is obviously that of providing for immediate
needs—food, fuel, clothing, shelter and medical supplies. While

the Food and Agriculture Organization (described in the next chapter) will deal with the long-term problems of agricultural development and improved nutritional standards, UNRRA must deal with emergency problems. Collaboration between the two bodies is, however, essential.

It is especially important that farmers be able to sow and harvest essential crops in the first crop year, to rehabilitate their farms and to build up their dairy herds. The early resumption of the fishing industry is important. Provision for the exchange of foodstuffs for industrial products needed by farmers at stabilized prices is essential to prevent hoarding. Thus transport and marketing enter into the food relief problem.

Local Industry

Public municipal utilities must be repaired to meet the immediate needs for urban living, including light, water, sanitation, power and transport. Local manufacture of food, clothing and medical supplies must be started as soon as possible. For all this, raw materials, machinery and spare parts will be needed.

Shelter

UNRRA cannot undertake to rebuild the devastated areas. But it must aid in providing for temporary shelter. Homes, hospitals and schools must be repaired. The need for temporary shelter in Russia and China will be very great.

Health and Medical Care

Health work is a primary responsibility of UNRRA. Infant mortality, tuberculosis and epidemics are major problems. "The seeds of disease," says Dr. Frank G. Boudreau, "have been sown all over Europe." There is danger of vast epidemics unless nations act together to cope adequately with this problem.

Welfare Services

One of the reports contained in "First Session of the Council of the United Nations Relief and Rehabilitation Administration: Selected Documents" is on welfare services and voluntary relief agencies. These welfare services involve provision for the personal rehabilitation of individuals requiring special help. The provision for food, clothing and shelter is not enough. The specific problems of individuals must be taken care of in order to bolster up individual responsibility and self-help. Many war veterans will need special care. War orphans present a problem of large magnitude. Welfare agencies and trained personnel in the field of social work must be used extensively to help meet these specific needs. The officials of UNRRA are aware of these problems and in co-operation with the various governments are prepared to enlist the support of voluntary relief agencies in the welfare field. Moreover, the private agencies themselves are awake to the problem. In Great Britain a consultative body has been formed, the Council of British Societies for Relief Abroad. In the United States the American Council of Voluntary Agencies for Foreign Service has been organized. These private organizations are prepared to operate under the general guidance of the Director General of the United Nations Relief and Rehabilitation Administration.

Displaced Populations

The problem of uprooted people is one of the urgent tasks confronting UNRRA. It is estimated that there are in Europe alone from 20 to 30 million displaced persons,[2] apart from war

[2] Cf. *Europe's Uprooted People: The Relocation of Dislocated Population*, No. 36, National Planning Association.

prisoners, while in China there is an approximately equal number. When hostilities cease, the repatriation, as far as possible, of these vast numbers will present almost insuperable problems.

It is clear that UNRRA must undertake large responsibility for the return of United Nations nationals to their own countries, both from liberated and conquered territories. In this important task UNRRA will work in close co-operation with other agencies such as the International Red Cross, the International Labor Office and the Intergovernmental Committee on Refugees.

The International Red Cross is especially concerned with prisoners of war. It has unique sources of information about prison camps, and it will play a leading part in the repatriation of war prisoners, working in association with the military authorities, with UNRRA and with the governments concerned.

In the event that the goal of full employment and high levels of income is realized in the postwar world, it is evident that the problem of relocating displaced persons will become feasible. If there is mass unemployment, the problem becomes virtually insoluble. With respect to the newer countries which may be able to attract immigrants, the problem of settlement and employment of uprooted peoples would be greatly facilitated if large-scale development projects are undertaken which would promote industrialization and diversification of agriculture. Here the International Bank for Reconstruction and Development can play an important role. The International Labor Organization has set up a Permanent Migration Committee. Consultation and co-operation between UNRRA and the ILO is envisaged.

UNRRA is an agency for the transition period. Long-run aspects of activities started by it will, however, be handed on to permanent agencies, including among others the International Labor Organization, the Food and Agriculture Organization, and the Bank for Reconstruction and Development.

CHAPTER XI

THE FOOD AND AGRICULTURE ORGANIZATION OF THE UNITED NATIONS

IN MAY, 1943, representatives of 44 governments met in Hot Springs, Virginia, upon the invitation of the government of the United States to consider ways and means of achieving the postwar goal of freedom from want. When the delegates left, the foundations of an international organization to deal with the problems of food and agriculture had been laid and an important forward step taken for a more effective and comprehensive attack, both on a national and on an international scale, on three of the great scourges of mankind: rural poverty, malnutrition and ill health.

The work accomplished at Hot Springs indicated the desirability of setting up a permanent international organization that could continuously deal with these problems. Many of the aspects that were considered by the Conference and on which recommendations were made have been neglected by the nations in the past. And even in those cases where the existence of these problems has been recognized, insufficient action has been taken.

The Conference stressed the urgent need for action and indicated the way in which desired results can be accomplished. It proposed the setting up of an organization that could provide the necessary information and assistance to governments in dealing with the problems involved.

The problems of health and prevention of disease are closely linked with the problems of adequate nutrition and better education. They, in turn, have an important bearing on agricultural production. In many cases the basic condition is that of poverty. Only a broad and comprehensive attack on all these related problems can hope to achieve results.

Not infrequently the situation is one that precludes effective isolated action by individual states. Agricultural production and consumption are peculiarly dependent upon world-wide markets. It is therefore of prime importance that an international organization should exist to deal with those problems that in scope transcend national boundaries and to assure that concerted and enlightened action will be taken by all the nations concerned.

While the long-run goals of increased agricultural production and adequate nutritional standards should never be lost sight of, the Conference was aware that the immediate postwar problems are of such an urgent nature that long-run adjustments might in some cases have to be delayed. In particular, it recommended that no restrictions be put on production during the immediate postwar period and that prime attention be directed toward removing the threat of starvation in large parts of the world. Transportation and distribution difficulties would be particularly acute during this period. These, however, are peculiarly the problems confronting UNRRA, which were discussed in the preceding chapter.

In the long run, the problems of health, nutrition and agricultural production must be attacked from several sides. Improved health facilities, education and provision for more adequate housing for the rural population are important aspects. An overwhelming portion of the world suffers from malnutrition. Even in the so-called rich countries of the world a considerable portion of the population is ill fed and has insufficient income to buy an adequate and healthful diet. As a first and important step in remedying this situation the Conference recommended adequate nutritional measures for the peculiarly vulnerable groups including pregnant and nursing women, children, adolescents and low-income sections of the population.

Simultaneously with these measures important steps must be taken looking toward a more efficient and stable agricultural production. This involves in many countries diversification of production, the undertaking of large agricultural improvement projects, the development of natural resources, and improvements in the processing, distribution and marketing of agricultural products.

In many cases the great poverty prevailing among the agricultural population is a consequence of overpopulation and inefficient production methods. Here diversification will help, supplemented by measures to provide better health and education for the agricultural population. Overpopulation calls basically for measures to control excessive rates of increase. In addition, much can be done by greater diversification of the economy and by finding opportunities for the industrial employment of excess farm populations.

The Conference set up several working committees which considered the broad problems of food and agriculture. The topics assigned to them were: Consumption Levels and Requirements, Expansion of Production and Adaptation to Consumption Needs, Facilitation and Improvement of Distribution, and Recommendations for Continuing and Carrying Forward the Work of the Conference. On the basis of the reports made by the technical sections, several recommendations and resolutions were adopted looking toward a solution of the agricultural and food problems facing the world both in the immediate postwar period and in the coming decades. An Interim

Commission was entrusted with the task of working out a plan for establishing a permanent organization.

In its first report of August, 1944, the Interim Commission presented a draft of the Constitution of the Food and Agriculture Organization of the United Nations to be submitted to the members of the Conference. The Constitution will become effective upon acceptance by 20 members.

The Constitution provides for a general Conference as the main organ of the new agency. The Conference will meet at least once a year and determine the policy of the Organization and agree by a two-thirds majority to discharge any additional functions consistent with the purposes of the Organization. Each member nation will be represented by one member.

The Conference will appoint an Executive Committee of 9 to 15 persons empowered to act in the intervals between the meetings of the Conference.

The current work of the Organization will be carried on by a Director-General, who will be the responsible head of the Organization, and an international staff with technical competence in the various branches of the work.

The international character of the Organization is stressed by absolving the staff from any responsibility that is not of an exclusively international character and that is not based on instructions of the Organization. Diplomatic privileges and immunities will be accorded to the Director-General and members of his staff.

Provision is made for close co-operation and agreements where it appears desirable between the Organization and other public international organizations with related responsibilities. When a general international organization for world security is set up, the Food and Agriculture Organization would be tied in, charged with responsibility in the special field of nutrition and agriculture.

The purposes of the Organization are stated in the Preamble

of the Constitution. The member nations agree to take action either separately or collectively to promote the common welfare and contribute toward an expanding world economy by raising levels of nutrition and standards of living of the people under their respective jurisdictions, by improving the efficiency of the production and distribution of all food and agricultural products, and by bettering the conditions of their rural populations.

The Conference at Hot Springs recognized that effective action taken by the states individually is the most important means of achieving the proposed goals, and several recommendations are directed to the states to that effect. In carrying out these recommendations, however, the states would be greatly benefited by an international organization which would be ready to give advice and assistance and be the instrument for co-ordinated and joint action by the states, whenever that proved necessary or desirable.

Article I of the Constitution describes the functions of the Organization. One important function will be the collection, analysis, interpretation and dissemination of information relating to nutrition, food and agriculture. Second, the Organization is charged with the task of promoting and recommending national and international action with respect to scientific, technological, social and economic research in these fields, the improvement of education and administration, and the spread of public knowledge of nutritional and agricultural science and practice. Third, it will be concerned with practical problems relating to the conservation of natural resources, the adoption of improved methods of agricultural production, the processing, marketing and distributing of products, provision of adequate national and international agricultural credit, and policies with respect to agricultural commodity arrangements. The Organization will be prepared to furnish technical assistance to governments upon request, and to organize in co-operation with the governments concerned missions to assist them in carrying out the recommendations of the Conference. The member nations, in turn, are requested to report periodically to the Organization on the progress made toward achieving the purposes set forth in the Preamble and on action taken on the basis of recommendations made by the Conference.

In addition to its own research and interpretation of data, the Organization will initiate and stimulate research throughout the world. The Organization will also function as a clearing agency of the various research agencies, co-ordinating their projects and procedures wherever possible. In many cases it will be merely a question of using more effectively such information and knowledge as is already available, adapting it to changing conditions or to particular situations.

The necessary research will cover a wide range of subjects in the field of the natural sciences, of technology, such as irrigation, drainage and other conservation measures, the economic aspects of agriculture and study of social factors such as the distribution of population between agriculture and industry, population movements, land tenure, food habits, rural housing and sanitation, rural schools and rural electrification.

An important field of investigation for the Organization will be the dissemination of the information and the promotion of education in fields relating to the Organization's work. Various types of publications issued by the Organization will serve this purpose, together with the promotion of wider circulation of established publications in these fields. The Organization will also advise and assist governments and educational institutions in planning courses and research.

The Organization will make recommendations to member countries. Such recommendations may call for the co-operative action of several members, and it is particularly in these cases that the Organization can perform useful work. These recommendations may range in form from formal agreements to be ratified by a large number of nations to resolutions embodying proposals for separate action.

The Organization may provide assistance to governments in working out programs for raising the nutritional level of the population, diversifying production, enlarging foreign markets, and in presenting the case for loans from international credit agencies such as the International Bank for Reconstruction and Development.

The work of the Organization will not be confined to agricultural food products. It will also include fisheries, forestry and nonfood agricultural products. Fisheries make up a considerable part of the world's food supply and will be particularly important in the immediate postwar years. In many countries forestry products supplement other farm products. Forestry problems are of such a nature that it is particularly important to consider them in world terms. Action on an international scale will need to be taken to prevent waste and uneconomical use of the forest resources of the world.

Nonfood agricultural products are an important part of the world's agricultural production. Some of them are necessities of life, others contribute significantly to human health and well-being. In several countries these products contribute the most important part of agricultural production and agricultural exports. Consumption of many of these commodities is particularly dependent upon fluctuations in general prosperity. It will be part of the task of the Organization not only to develop and secure more complete information on the consumption and effective demand for these products in different countries but also to help broaden their uses.

The International Bank for Reconstruction and Development can play an important role in making available adequate funds for agricultural projects. The Food and Agriculture Organization can offer expert advice and make recommendations to the Bank in that field. International agricultural credit can make an important contribution to the stability and expansion of the world economy. Investments of this type are likely to yield quicker returns than in many other fields. Agricultural credit in this connection must be interpreted in a broad sense to include not only its traditional forms, such as credit for land reclamation, irrigation, marketing facilities, but also credit for adjustments in other parts of the economy in the interest of agricultural diversification and reorientation.

More productive and efficient agriculture and more adequate nutrition are in themselves an important step in providing economic stability and an expanding world economy. But the Food Conference in its reports and recommendations has constantly stressed the fact that in order to carry out adequately the measures that have been mentioned, it is necessary to insure a favorable general economic environment. Only in an expanding world economy of full employment is there any likelihood that agricultural policies can become fully effective. The measures in the field of agriculture have therefore to be coordinated with other measures directed toward expansion. Full employment and rising productivity in the urban communities are essential to provide the necessary purchasing power to insure adequate markets for agriculture. And improved living standards for the rural population, achieved through greater efficiency, better education, health and nutrition, can in turn contribute much to general economic stability and expansion. On this basis world trade would prosper and a wider distribution of agricultural products could be achieved. This involves a considerable measure of interdependence and this can only be safeguarded by an adequate international security organization.

CHAPTER XII

INTERNATIONAL COMMODITY AGREEMENTS AND BUFFER STOCKS

CONSIDERABLE attention has recently been directed to the future of international cartels and other business combines. In this connection it is important to consider the role and function of international commodity agreements. Some industrial cartels should certainly be suppressed, while others should be controlled.[1] And international commodity arrangements, in so far as they may prove necessary to meet urgent problems, should be managed so as to promote social, and not antisocial, ends.

Since agriculture is the major field in which these arrangements are most likely to play a role, this chapter will deal with agricultural commodities, although some of the considerations and findings are relevant also for other raw-material agreements.

Agricultural Maladjustments

In many respects agricultural commodities present problems of their own. Agricultural production is exposed to seasonal changes and weather hazards. Bumper crops or droughts may cause sharp short-run fluctuations of prices. Such cases present no problem of serious long-run maladjustments but only of temporary distress. Cyclical fluctuations of income and employment have international repercussions and are likely to

---

[1] *See* Chapter XXI, "Monopoly and International Cartels," in this book.

weigh with particular force on the position of primary-producing countries. Finally, serious structural changes in the supply and demand for agricultural products have occurred on a large scale. These maladjustments are often of international scope and cannot be dealt with effectively by the independent action of individual countries.

Governmental action, national and international, could be directed toward smoothing out fluctuations, softening their impact both on producers and consumers and bringing about greater stability in market conditions. While the desirability of action along those lines is generally conceded, there is disagreement as to the nature and scope of international arrangements. In addition, doubts have been expressed whether such arrangements can deal effectively with some of the deeper-lying causes of these maladjustments, and whether the dangers and abuses to which they are open are not likely to preserve and worsen, instead of correcting, the situation that called for governmental action.

Views of the Hot Springs Conference

The Hot Springs Conference on Food and Agriculture devoted considerable attention to the question of international commodity arrangements. The Conference was concerned with a better distribution of agricultural products on an international scale in order to promote increased food consumption and more adequate nutrition. It recognized that international commodity arrangements may play a useful part in the world economy but suggested further study to determine the precise form that such arrangements should take and the extent to which regulation of production may be needed.

In its first report, the Interim Commission on Food and Agriculture stressed the important role of such arrangements for co-ordinating and adjusting conflicts in the price and marketing policies of various nations. Such arrangements, it was thought, might mitigate fluctuations in prices and help to maintain adequate supplies to consumers at all times, while securing expanding markets to producers and promoting desirable adjustments in agricultural production.

In line with the findings and recommendations of the Hot Springs Conference, the Interim Commission recommended that a special international conference meet at an early date to consider and agree upon a body of principles that would be applicable to all international commodity arrangements. The Conference should establish an international authority or agency which would review the application of these principles to individual agreements and supervise their administration. The agency would be in charge of arrangements with regard to both agricultural and nonagricultural products. Since the broad aims of agricultural arrangements are related to its general goals the Food and Agriculture Organization should participate in this international agency. In my own writings I have urged the establishment of such an agency under the title International Commodity Corporation.[2]

Opposing Viewpoints

The discussion at the Food and Agriculture Conference disclosed differences of opinion with regard to the proper scope and function of commodity agreements. Two views gained considerable attention. The British delegation strongly favored agreements for accumulating and holding buffer stocks of the most important agricultural commodities. According to their view such arrangements would stabilize the market for individual commodities, not by imposing export and production quotas but by setting a price in advance at which production

---

[2] *See* my article on "World Institutions for Stability and Expansion," *Foreign Affairs*, January, 1944.

and consumption could be equalized. An international body would be ready to purchase any excess production that might occur in one year and would dispose of such stocks in years of scarcity. Thus demand and supply would be equalized, not annually but over a number of years. Such an agency would also endeavor to maintain an adequate reserve of commodities at all times. Price adjustments would be made to bring production and consumption into balance.[3]

Such arrangements would not aim at maintaining fixed prices but would seek to eliminate deviations from the long-term trend. According to this view quantitative controls should be used only in exceptional cases since they tend to keep production at a low level in order to insure abnormally high prices.

To meet short-run fluctuations, quantitative controls are unnecessary since such temporary maladjustments could be met by buffer stocks. In the case of long-term disequilibrium, quantitative controls may appear to be necessary but they may endanger the perpetuation of the status quo. In those cases in which quantitative controls may need to be adopted, they should be devised so as to guard against restrictive tendencies and to hasten the process of long-run adjustment.

Against this opinion it was maintained that buffer stock arrangements without production control are not adequate. If quantitative controls have been open to objections in the past this, it was urged, was mainly due to the fact that they were established at the bottom of the depression when the position of the co-operating countries was already desperate. Accordingly, the arrangements were almost of necessity of a severely restrictive type. Attention in the future should be concentrated on increasing production by pursuing expansionist policies and capturing new markets. Efforts in this direction would be facilitated by adequate consumer representation.

[3] For a more detailed discussion of these problems *see* J. D. Black and S. S. Tsou, "International Commodity Arrangements," *Quarterly Journal of Economics*, August, 1944.

Existing Commodity Agreements

In view of the wide range of opinion and the complexity of the problems involved, it may be desirable to review briefly the nature of agricultural commodity agreements existing at the present time.

The most important and elaborate is the wheat agreement entered into in June, 1942. It supersedes the one established in 1933 between nine wheat-exporting countries and twelve importing countries. The members of the present agreement are the big exporters, the United States, Canada, Australia and Argentina, and one importing country, the United Kingdom.

After taking into account the exports of the nonparticipating nations it was agreed to divide the export market by allocating to each member a certain quota of the total. In addition to quotas for current exports the countries agreed also to hold reserve stocks at the end of each crop year which should not fall below certain minima or exceed certain maximum limits set for each country. Each member country agreed to adopt measures to insure that the production in its territory shall not exceed the quantity needed for domestic requirements, the basic export quotas and the maximum reserve stocks. Surpluses must be disposed of within the country.

Each August a basic minimum and maximum price is to be established for one year and sales must take place within that range. The criteria that determine the price range are stated rather vaguely. The prices should provide for a reasonable remuneration to producers in exporting countries, should be fair to consumers in importing countries and, after making appropriate allowance for exchange and transportation costs, should stand in a reasonable relationship to the prices of other commodities.

All five countries agreed to contribute a pool of 100 million bushels without compensation for relief of war-stricken countries and other areas in need. Furthermore the contracting governments agreed to take steps leading to a wider consumption of wheat in importing countries by lowering tariffs on the products those countries must export. The present agreement remains in force until two years after the end of the war with Japan or until a new agreement is set up.

The Inter-American Coffee Agreement signed in 1940 provides for the division of the United States' import quota among the South and Central American countries and allocates exports to other countries. The structure of the agreement is determined by the presence of one big importing country, the United States, and one big exporting country, Brazil. No price provisions are included in the agreement. In some cases rigid production controls have been instituted. At the present time the United States' price is fixed by OPA price regulation but is expected to rise as soon as the ceiling prices are removed.

The Sugar Agreement of 1937 includes both the principal exporting countries and important importing countries. The purpose of the agreement was to establish export quotas and limitations as to stocks for the exporting countries. The importing countries in turn agreed not to use artificial measures to expand their own sugar production. This would give exporting countries the benefit of any increases in demand.

This agreement in operation encountered serious obstacles. The main problem relates to the competition between the low-cost cane-sugar-producing countries and the artificially supported higher cost beet-sugar production of the importing countries. The agreement has not been very effective in its attempts to control total production.

Another agricultural commodity agreement in force at the present time is the beef agreement between the United Kingdom, the most important beef-importing country, and its suppliers. Its purpose is to stabilize imports and keep prices steady. The total imports into the United Kingdom are divided between the member exporting countries.

Difficulties and Abuses

These experiences show clearly the difficulties and abuses to which commodity agreements are exposed. The price is usually fixed under the influence of the producing groups and is therefore likely to be established at a higher level than the long-term market situation would warrant.

The establishment of export quotas aims to prevent ruinous competition between the exporting countries, but the production control is often ineffective. When attempts to reduce production are made on an international or national scale, the cutback usually takes place on a historical basis, allowing each producer a percentage of his past production in the base year. Such an approach is undesirable because it takes no account of change. Inefficient production is maintained.

Despite these drawbacks international commodity arrangements may perform a useful function. Their role in the postwar period will depend largely upon the general economic and political conditions that will prevail and upon the measures that governments will be prepared to take to remove or minimize their objectionable features. Commodity agreements cannot be the answer to fundamental maladjustments. But they can play an important role while energetic action is taken to remove basic maladjustments.

Several suggestions have been made to strengthen the usefulness of commodity agreements in the postwar period. Prices should be set in such a way as to bring production and consumption into balance. In those cases where producing groups may be in need of support, supplementary income payments should be coupled with inducements to make production adjustments that promote efficiency.

Expansionist economic policies pursued by the major countries would provide the best atmosphere in which adjustments could be made. Indeed, if high levels of income and employment can be maintained, the need for the adjustment of agricultural production would be greatly reduced since the demand for agricultural commodities rises with increasing national income. Expansionist policies would also broaden the international markets of the agricultural importing countries. Accordingly, they would be able to shift out of high-cost agricultural production to more productive occupations. Economic expansion and rising living standards would promote a freer international commodity flow.

If adequate measures are taken to achieve full employment and high levels of world trade, commodity agreements can serve constructive ends. They could become useful instruments to achieve international stability by facilitating needed structural adjustments, by promoting a wider distribution of products, by discovering new production outlets and by measures to minimize short-term price instability.

International Commodity Corporation

To integrate the stabilization and adjustment programs of separate commodity agreements it would be desirable to set up, as we have noted above, an International Commodity Corporation designed to buy, store and sell international raw materials and to act as a buffer in the raw-material market. In the event that a deflation of raw-material prices were impending, the Corporation should make large purchases of storable raw materials. It would permit the free play of market-price forces within upper and lower price ranges for each commodity. Buying operations would be indicated as soon as the price pierced the lower limit, and selling operations as soon as it rose above the upper limit. These upper and lower limits should be the subject of continuous study by the Corporation and should be adjusted from time to time according to fundamental trends of demand and supply. An important part of the Corporation's function would be to search for new uses for basic raw materials and to co-operate with the various national governments to facilitate the movement of resources out of submarginal areas in an effort to adjust supply to long-run changes in demand.

Such a corporation or agency would be acceptable only if it constituted a part of a general program of international economic co-operation and development. Independently of such a program there is danger that the Corporation, together with the related specialized commodity arrangements, might not give sufficient attention to the expansionist and developmental aspects without which no solution can be found for the basic problem of agricultural adjustment.

CHAPTER XIII

THE INTERNATIONAL LABOR ORGANIZATION

THE International Labor Organization has by now had a quarter century of useful experience. It has made a notable contribution to international co-operation in an important area of economic life. It is the one official agency through which labor and employers participate directly in the making of international policy. It held its twenty-sixth session in Philadelphia in May, 1944.

Fundamental Principles of the ILO

The conference reaffirmed the fundamental principles on which the ILO is based. In somewhat abbreviated form they are:

1. Labor is not a commodity.
2. Freedom of expression and of association are essential to sustained progress.
3. The war against want requires concerted international effort in which representatives of workers and employees, enjoying equal status with those of governments, join in free discussion and democratic decision.

The conference proclaimed that lasting peace can be established only if it is based on social justice. It therefore affirmed the right to economic security and equal opportunity for all human beings irrespective of race, creed or sex. The conference disclosed that it must be a central aim of national and international policy to attain conditions necessary for such security and equality.

The ILO recognizes its obligation to promote measures looking toward the improvement of labor conditions throughout the world. This involves, specifically, policies in regard to wages and earnings, hours and other conditions of work, including a minimum living wage. It involves the recognition of the right of collective bargaining, and the co-operation of management and labor in the continuous improvement of productive efficiency. It involves, moreover, the extension of social security, adequate protection for the life and health of workers in all occupations, a comprehensive program of medical care, provisions for child welfare and maternity protection, adequate nutrition, housing, and facilities for recreation and culture, and the assurance of educational and vocational opportunity.

The conference recognized that these things cannot adequately be accomplished except within the framework of full employment and ever increasing productivity. Accordingly, the conference urged the importance of fuller and broader utilization of the world's productive resources. It recognized that the objectives set forth cannot be achieved without effective international and national action, including measures to expand production and consumption and to avoid severe economic fluctuations. It recognized that its goals require the economic and social advancement of the less developed regions of the world and a greater stability in world prices of primary products. It called for a high and steady volume of international trade and pledged the fullest co-operation of the ILO with other bodies entrusted with responsibility for this task. And finally it pledged its full co-operation for the promotion of the health, education and well-being of all peoples. The conference gave to the world a telling slogan which will not soon be forgotten: "Poverty anywhere constitutes a danger to prosperity everywhere."

The conference recognized that while the principles which it affirmed are applicable to all peoples everywhere, the manner of their application must be determined with due regard to the stage of social and economic development reached in each country. Nevertheless, it affirmed the belief that the progressive application of these principles to all peoples as rapidly as possible is a matter of concern to the whole civilized world.

Social Policy

In order to carry out by specific measures the broad objectives set forth above, the conference set out a number of guides for social policy. I shall not enumerate these in detail, but they involve among other things the following:

1. *Income security:* Income-security schemes must be adopted to relieve want and destitution. Income security should be organized as far as possible on the basis of compulsory social security. Provision for needs not covered by social security should be made by social assistance to dependent children, needy invalids, aged persons and other persons in want.

2. *Contingencies covered:* The range of contingencies to be covered by social insurance should embrace all contingencies in which an insured person is prevented from earning his living. These include unemployment, old age, death of the bread-winner, employment injuries, disability, sickness and maternity. Supplements for the first two children should be added to all benefits for loss of earnings, and provision for further children should be made by means of children's allowances.

3. *Social assistance:* Society should co-operate with parents through general measures of assistance designed to secure the well-being of dependent children. Invalids, aged persons and widows not receiving social-insurance benefits, and whose incomes do not exceed a prescribed level, should be entitled to special maintenance allowances. Allowances should, moreover, be provided for all persons who are in want.

4. *Public health:* The conference report devoted a great deal of space to medical care. Medical or health centers should be established where the population and number of beneficiaries justify a program to care for the health of the area. Areas with scattered populations and remote from towns or cities should be provided with traveling clinics in motor vans or aircraft equipped to furnish first aid, dental treatment, general examinations, and maternal and infant health services.

Employment in the Transition from War to Peace

The conference adopted recommendations dealing with employment in the transition period. These included measures with respect to the collection of information about the probable demand for workers in the main industries and occupations under conditions of full employment, the educational and occupational background of workers, the demobilization of the armed forces, industrial reconversion, vocational guidance, retraining programs, geographical mobility, the employment of young workers, the employment of women, the employment of disabled workers, the regularization of employment in particular industries, the employment service, and the planning of public works in the transition so as to assure the prompt and orderly use of human and natural resources.

With respect to immediate postwar policies, the conference took note of the need of an orderly and efficient demobilization program, the adoption of fiscal programs to check both inflation and deflation, the maintenance of adequate demand through monetary and fiscal measures, and the improvement of collective-bargaining procedures.

Migration Problems

In the interwar period the ILO was dealing continuously with migration problems. At a conference in 1938 of 10 European emigration countries and 8 Latin-American immigration countries, the conclusion was reached that a major obstacle to orderly and desirable migration was the lack of financial resources on the part both of the country of emigration and that of immigration. In order to help finance orderly and desirable migration, the ILO decided to establish a Permanent Committee on Migration for Settlement. This project, while interrupted by the war, has not been abandoned. At the Philadelphia conference in May, 1944, the Governing Body of the ILO decided to change the name of the Committee to Permanent Migration Committee so as to broaden the scope to include all kinds of migration, not merely migration for settlement in new countries. The ILO plans to convene the Committee as soon as circumstances permit. A proposal was, moreover, made for the exchange of data between national employment services providing migrant labor and displaced persons with the best available information concerning employment opportunities in various countries.

International Policies

The conference adopted resolutions concerning social provisions in the peace settlement, international policies relating to the repatriation of prisoners and displaced persons, the orderly migration of labor, international monetary arrangements, international loans, commercial policies, national full-employment policies, taxation, monopolistic practices, encouragement of private investment, internationally financed developmental works, and co-operation in regard to the preparation of plans for public works in occupied countries.

Much attention was devoted to the problems of the occupied countries following their liberation. It was pointed out by a representative from France that for these countries "it will not be a matter merely of transition from war to a peace economy. It will be a matter of real economic and social reconstruction." A resolution was adopted asserting the determination of the ILO to assist in rebuilding the social life of these countries "according to principles of international solidarity and respect for the fundamental spiritual and human values."

The conference recommended that member countries shall take steps to promote the well-being and development of peoples of dependent territories and to encourage the desire on their part for social progress. Every effort should be made to secure, on an international, regional, national or territorial basis, financial and technical assistance in the economic development of dependent territories in such a way as to safeguard the interests of the peoples living in such areas. All possible steps should be taken by appropriate international, regional, national and territorial measures to promote improvement in such fields as public health, housing, nutrition, education, the welfare of children, the status of women, condition of employment, the remuneration of wage earners, social security and standards of public services. Steps should be taken to assist these peoples in the framing and execution of measures of social progress, preferably through their own elected representatives where possible.

Conclusion

The International Labor Organization has played a useful role in the last 25 years. Through its research activities and publications it has greatly increased our knowledge about labor conditions throughout the world. During the period of its existence immense progress has been made in labor legislation, in collective bargaining and in social security. The ILO has done much to promote these ends. Being founded upon the active collaboration of employer groups and labor groups as well as of governments, it is firmly rooted in practical policy. Organized as it is, in this tripartite representation, it promotes good labor relations between employers and employees, while at the same time it works through government when private voluntary action proves inadequate. In this manner, public policy with respect to matters concerning labor and labor relations is guided by those whose separate and mutual interests are most at stake.

CHAPTER XIV

The Economic and Social Council of the World Security Organization

The Dumbarton Oaks Conference (August 21 to October 7, 1944) proposed the establishment of a general international organization for world security under the title of the United Nations. The broad objective of this organization is to maintain the peace of the world.

The general international organization would include (*a*) a General Assembly, (*b*) a Security Council, (*c*) an international Court of Justice and (*d*) an Economic and Social Council.

The political, military and security aspects of the Dumbarton Oaks Conference fall outside the scope of this volume. I shall limit myself, therefore, to a discussion of the functions of the Economic and Social Council.

The Economic and Social Council would serve as a link between the General Assembly and the various international economic organizations (such as those discussed in preceding chapters of this book). It would be the means of effecting co-ordinated and integrated action between those various agencies.

The Dumbarton Oaks proposal stresses the need for creating conditions of stability and well-being necessary for peaceful and friendly relations among nations. This involves the solution of international economic, social and other humanitarian problems. The responsibility for these problems is vested in the General Assembly and, under its authority, in the Economic and Social Council.

The Economic and Social Council should make recommendations on its own initiative with respect to international economic, social and humanitarian matters. It should receive and consider reports from the various international economic and other organizations and co-ordinate their activities through consultations with, and recommendations to, such agencies.

It is proposed that the Economic and Social Council set up an Economic Commission, a Social Commission, and such other commissions as may be required. These commissions should consist of a permanent staff of experts which would constitute a part of the secretariat of the General Assembly.

The Economic and Social Council would be expected to make arrangements for representatives of the various economic and other organizations to participate in its deliberations and in those of the commissions established by it. On the other side, the Economic and Social Council may make arrangements to participate in the policy making of the various international economic institutions through informal contact with their governing boards.

The urgent need of a co-ordinating Economic and Social Council is evident from the experience of the interwar period. In that period there was virtually no co-operation between governments in their efforts to cope with the problems of the great depression. Each country seized upon opportunistic measures to alleviate the situation. There was no regard for the effect of these unilateral policies upon other countries. Often the measures used were detrimental to other countries and called forth retaliatory action. Thus the unilateral policies pursued often made matters worse instead of better. There was no effort to fight a common foe together.

We know that depressions are contagious and spread from country to country. We also know that if one country attempts an expansionist program all alone it is likely to find itself in balance of payment difficulties. If it persistently pursues its policy of expansion, it may accordingly be compelled to insulate its economy from the outside world. This will lead to highly restrictive trade and exchange measures which are destructive of international trade and international prosperity.

Accordingly, it is important that countries move along together in a co-ordinated manner in their antidepression policies. No country, if it expects to remain a good neighbor in the family of nations, can go it alone. "If we do not hang together, we shall hang separately."

The unfortunate consequences of separatist and unilateral action in the interwar period need not be repeated. The unhappy results then experienced could largely be avoided if co-ordinated expansionist policies were undertaken, especially by the larger industrial nations.

All this does not mean that every country must be straitjacketed into a uniform pattern to which all must conform. There may be large and important differences in the methods employed to attain high levels of income and employment in the various countries. What is important is timing and direction. If co-ordinated action is taken, then the program of each country will be reinforced and strengthened by the general expansion occurring elsewhere. Thus international balance can be preserved and the prosperity of the world as a whole encouraged and maintained.

Each of the various economic institutions that I have discussed in the preceding chapters is concerned with special phases of international stability, high employment, world prosperity and high living standards. Each constitutes a part of a larger problem. The job of each is interrelated to that of the others.

The functions of the Bank for Reconstruction and Development sustain and reinforce those of the International Monetary Fund, and vice versa. The educational and technical work of the Food and Agriculture Organization is basic to the developmental activities of the Bank. The activities of the International Commodity Corporation affect the balance of payment problems confronting the International Monetary Fund. The same holds for the International Trade Authority. Thus it goes on and on. The jobs to be done are highly specialized and must be performed by specialized agencies. But they are interrelated. If each reinforces the other in a co-ordinated attack on inflation or deflation, in the promotion of high employment and rising living standards, and in securing international stability and prosperity, the combined effect can be very great. But this requires co-ordination.

All this implies the need not only for the separate economic organizations but also for an over-all Economic and Social Council which can view the problem as a whole. The central aim and responsibility of such an over-all council should be the promotion of high employment and international stability throughout the world. The specialized organizations could, each in its particular assignment, yet in concerted action, contribute much toward a high and stable level of world economic activity.

Finally, it should be emphasized that the Economic and Social Council is not intended to be merely a co-ordinating body. It should assume direct responsibility for the initiation and carrying through of a program which the general welfare of the family of nations may require. The Economic and Social Council should assume a vigorous leadership in the formation of policies broadly relating to economic, social and other humanitarian matters in the international sphere.

PART THREE

EXPORTS, IMPORTS AND DOMESTIC
FULL EMPLOYMENT

CHAPTER XV

Can the United States Compete in World Markets?

Whenever international problems are under discussion in public forums one question inevitably pops out. How can the American exporter hope to compete in the world markets against foreign competitors in view of our high wage rates and many other adverse factors?

To this perennial and oft-repeated question, any economist who is conversant with the facts of our foreign trade during the last quarter century is compelled to give the following comment. Far from being unable to compete in the world markets, the fact is that the United States competes altogether too well. We are always selling too much in the world markets. This indeed constitutes one of the great world problems. We are always selling to foreigners more than they are able to pay for. We are unwilling to purchase from foreigners enough to balance our trade. Hence the "world shortage of dollars." Unable to obtain payment in dollars, our exporters have time and again accumulated balances in foreign countries that they cannot convert into dollars. To some extent foreigners have made payment by shipping us gold. To some extent they have made payment by selling us bonds that turned sour. We have, in fact, shipped to the outside world in the last quarter century billions of dollars for which we have gotten no adequate return.

This is the record, broadly speaking, of our trade relations with the outside world during the last 25 years. There is clearly something wrong. But certainly what is wrong is not that we are not able to compete in the markets of the world. We oversell our product. Indeed it is precisely with respect to those products that are most in demand wherever living standards rise above a subsistence level that American industry excells. American producers with their mass-production techniques can undersell any competitor in automobiles, radios, typewriters, electric household appliances, washing machines, etc. These are just the things that all the world wants. American products are demanded everywhere. Indeed, foreigners want them so badly that they are always buying more than they can pay for. They cannot pay for them in dollars because we do not import enough in return.

Now the fact that we are always selling too much to the outside world is a major cause of world disequilibrium and has been for the last quarter century. It is one of the most serious international economic problems of our times. If we are to have a stable international world, this problem must somehow be solved. We cannot solve it by the old techniques. We need new policies and new international arrangements.

Nevertheless, the instinct of the businessman, who is looking for more exports, is fundamentally sound. The doctrinaire economist has often chided the businessman for his interest in exports. The doctrinaire economist has been inclined to say: Why not produce for our own people instead of making goods for foreigners for which as a nation we are frequently ill paid or paid not at all? Indeed, the only way in which we can as a nation be paid for our exports is to import.

The businessman's viewpoint is sound in the respect that he wants to expand his business and to provide more employment for his workers. When his workers are employed, they in turn can buy more from other American industries. Thus exports do tend to increase prosperity, employment and real income. Exports do put people to work, raise purchasing power and promote business activity.

The conflict between the practical businessman and the doctrinaire economist will come up for more thorough and detailed discussion later. But at this point I wish to consider some of the international aspects of the "export approach" to internal prosperity. The measures frequently advocated to increase the exports of our country may have a seriously adverse effect upon other countries. Whether this in the final analysis hurts us or not depends upon whether the repercussions of our adverse action upon the outside world sooner or later reflect back upon ourselves with more or less disastrous consequences. From the standpoint of our own self-interest this is the important question.

The various measures to achieve internal prosperity by pushing exports have in recent economic literature been labeled "beggar my neighbor" policies. This phrase indicates that such means to achieve internal prosperity is won at the expense of our neighbors. We make them beggars while enriching ourselves.

One of the means to push exports is subsidy. Innumerable proposals have been made in Congress to provide subsidies in one way or another for the export of farm products. If more is exported, even at a low price, the remaining supply can sell at a much higher price in the internal market. The higher internal price in a large domestic market may more than offset the loss on relatively small exports in the foreign markets.

Another method to stimulate exports is "dumping." Industries with large capacities, unable to develop adequate sales volume at home, may dump their surplus products at cutthroat competitive prices in foreign markets. Restricted production for the home market insures a high internal price. The external price, while low, may nevertheless bring a return in excess of the small added cost of producing that portion of the product which is exported.

Exchange depreciation is another device to increase exports. If we reduce the foreign-exchange value of the dollar to a point below its true value (the so-called equilibrium rate) exports are stimulated. This can quite readily be seen from the following illustration. If the true value of the dollar in terms of the British monetary unit is $4.00, this means that a product selling competitively for one pound sterling in England should similarly sell for $4.00 in the United States. Now if we artificially depreciate the dollar so that $6.00 can be gotten in the foreign-exchange markets for one British pound, what then? Clearly the American exporter can still sell his product for one pound in the British market for which he now gets $6.00. This gives him a great advantage against English competitors. In order to push his product in England, he may now choose to sell for 16 shillings instead of as formerly at 20 shillings or one pound. But these 16 shillings will bring him at the depreciated dollar-sterling exchange rate $4.80. At the same time that he is undercutting his English competitor by 20 per cent, he is nevertheless getting, because of the depreciated exchange, $4.80 for his product instead of the former price of $4.00.

All these methods—and there are many others—of artificially stimulating exports clearly tend to drive the foreign producer out of business. While American exports and American employment in consequence of such tactics may rise, foreign employment tends to decline. Thus our prosperity is won at the expense of foreign producers and foreign workers. While curing our unemployment, we intensify theirs. Evidently this is not a good-neighbor policy. It is a policy by which we make "beggars" of other countries.

These policies lead to economic warfare. Other nations do not take the beating lying down. They retaliate in kind.

Between the two world wars, economic history is replete with innumerable examples of the use of these "fighting methods" and the backfire they have drawn from the injured country. It is not a pretty picture, but this is the kind of international world we have been living in. And it is usually not easy to find out "who started it."

The retaliation usually takes the form in one way or another of preventing the guilty country from achieving the exports it seeks. This may be done by raising tariffs and choking off imports from the offending country, or it may be done by "exchange control." Exchange control means that businessmen who wish to import are permitted to obtain only a limited and controlled amount of foreign exchange. Thus if a foreign country introduces exchange control against the United States, this means that its importers can get only a limited supply of "dollars" with which to pay the American exporter.

Another device to limit imports is to impose a fixed quantity on the amount that may be imported. Once this quota is filled in any given year no more can be imported. In this event, if these import quotas are directed against the United States, the American exporter would find his foreign market severely curtailed.

Thus when economic warfare is resorted to, the weapons that are employed are both "offensive" and "defensive." The "offensive" weapons are those that act artificially to push out exports. The country suffering from the ensuing cutthroat competition devises "defensive" weapons to ward off these offending exports and to prevent them from demoralizing its markets. The defending country, in other words, devises fighting weapons to limit the imports that may enter its borders.

This unhappy economic strife, as offensive tactics are met by retaliation, more and more destroys world trade.

To reach a workable international world it is evident that economic warfare needs to be supplanted by international collaboration. This means that nations must somehow learn to work together collectively to promote in the first instance internal prosperity and full employment and in the second instance such exchange of goods as is required to reach the highest possible standard of living. International collaboration can be developed so as to minimize economic warfare and to promote full employment, world prosperity and world trade.

CHAPTER XVI

CAN LEND-LEASE BE CONTINUED
INDEFINITELY?

WE HAVE seen in the preceding chapter that the policy of pushing exports upon other countries by export subsidy, exchange depreciation and similar measures tends to cure unemployment in the United States through the internationally immoral process of increasing unemployment in other countries. Naturally, other countries do not sit idly by while we are exporting unemployment to them, and, as we have seen, retaliations occur. Thus the end effect upon our own country of such a policy is likely to prove an unhappy one. Export subsidies may be met by countersubsidies, and currency depreciation may be met by competitive depreciation. Moreover, exchange control, import quotas or tariffs may impede our effort to push exports artificially upon other countries. In other words, the "beggar my neighbor" policy, when all the repercussions are taken account of, does not work.

But if this is the case, why not devise other means to stimulate exports without the unhappy consequences referred to? Various solutions have been proposed. While certain of these proposals rarely divulge their inner secret—in other words, rarely label themselves as schemes to make gifts to foreigners—this is, in fact, what they are.

One such proposal, indeed, may be regarded as openly frank with respect to its true nature. It has sometimes been proposed that we ought to continue beyond the immediate temporary period of relief and rehabilitation a long-range lend-lease program. It is sometimes argued that this is the only truly realistic approach. We know it to be a fact that in World War I and in the interwar period that followed we exported some $25 billion worth of goods which were financed partly by intergovernmental loans and partly by private loans. But in the final analysis the intergovernmental war loans were defaulted and a very large portion of the private loans suffered the same fate. Thus what had been thought to be loans turned out, in fact, to be gifts. The gifts came in part from the United States Treasury and in part from the pockets of private investors who had simply been fooled into thinking they were investing their money.

So far as the war expenditures are concerned, by common consent the lend-lease agreement is far superior to the intergovernmental war loans of World War I. We learned from that unhappy experience that such intergovernmental war debts are so disturbing to the world economy that they had better not be paid. And there had better be no pretense of payment.

The lend-lease plan was a brilliant way of solving this problem. Through lend-lease the war effort, in fact, became a co-operative effort in which each ally contributed to its utmost ability without attempting the commercial accounting we used in World War I with such disastrous consequences. To be sure, some settlement of accounts will be made under lend-lease, but certainly not in terms of the financial accounting involved in the making of regular financial loans.

Now it is argued that if, in fact, the United States wishes to export in excess of its imports in order to promote prosperity and employment in the United States, why not recognize the stark realities in the case and provide an indefinite program of lend-lease? If we are unwilling to take goods from foreign countries (our own industries being eager to produce almost everything that we consume ourselves) and if at the same time we want to export, then we had better face the realities and recognize things for what they are. We had better, it is said, give our goods away. We had better openly play Santa Claus.

Those who urge this point of view usually admit that it is really politically unfeasible. The argument is frequently advanced as a means of showing up the paradoxes and absurdities in our international position. We want to export but we will not permit foreigners to pay us for our exports since we refuse to buy goods and services in return. We want to export and we wish to pretend that we will get paid, though in fact experience shows that payment cannot be made.

More subtle ways of advancing the same solution have, however, been proposed. It has been suggested that as our exports exceed our imports, accumulating balances owing to the United States should after a certain period be canceled. The American exporters would, indeed, be paid immediately upon making the export through funds supplied by the Treasury or the Federal Reserve System. This is, in effect, what happens when foreigners pay us for excess exports in the form of gold. The gold is purchased by the Treasury and thus dollars are made available to foreigners with which to pay for the excess American exports. To be sure, the Treasury has obtained gold, but buried in Fort Knox it is of doubtful real value. It is, of course, true that the Treasury can very neatly get out of its own difficulty by depositing the gold, or rather gold certificates or gold-certificate credits, with the Federal Reserve Banks, thereby receiving in return a balance at the Federal Reserve Banks. By so doing, the excess of American exports is financed not by the taxpayer but by an extension of Federal Reserve credit. It is, in fact, paid for by a multiplication of the money supply.

It is not to be wondered at that the gold-purchase business, as a means of financing excess American exports, looks like hocus-pocus to many people. Some would prefer to go straight to the heart of the problem and finance excess American exports through an expansion of Federal Reserve credit without buying the gold and storing it away in Fort Knox. The effect on the money and banking system would be precisely the same as in the case of the gold purchases. The hocus-pocus is removed and we go straight to the problem of satisfying our desire for excess exports in the painless manner of expanding Federal Reserve credit.

Those who have suggested this remedy for the solution of our dilemma are probably at least halfway joking. The more cynical ones are merely getting amusement out of the analysis in order to bring discomfort to the ardent supporter of American export surpluses. But some would urge that the proposal is at any rate better than nothing as a solution for mass unemployment. If we do not have the wit to solve this problem by sensible measures, then useful exports to foreigners, though we get no adequate *quid pro quo* in return, are (so runs the argument) to be preferred to pyramid building or to mass unemployment.

The exchange of goods against gold was referred to above as senseless at least for the United States in view of its vast gold holdings. It is often said that the gold imports of the thirties were utterly useless. But this is, I think, an exaggeration. I shall discuss this at some length in the chapter that follows. It can, I believe, be shown that we did get some benefits from the gold imports, though from the world standpoint it was an unhappy experience. Moreover, whatever benefits we derived could have been had in a more rational manner. But it takes a very sophisticated country to be truly rational when it comes to money matters.

CHAPTER XVII

GOLD, EXPORTS AND LIQUIDITY

THE subject of money continues to be, in the minds of most people, a paradox. And now that the United States has accumulated $21 billion worth of gold and has buried a large stock in the vaults of Kentucky, not permitting the public or even the banks to hold it, the role played by gold in our modern economy is felt—as is quite understandable—to be more paradoxical than ever.[1]

The development of deposit banking has enhanced the mysticism surrounding money. Bankers, by supplying a medium of exchange (demand deposits), based formerly on a small metallic reserve but now on a credit obligation of the Federal Reserve Banks, appear to have performed a mysterious sleight of hand. Even the Federal Reserve Banks no longer hold gold—only gold-certificate credits.

Time was when the role of gold in the money system was simple and direct. Then the precious metals formed the chief means of payment. But under the development of commercial banking, deposit currency, bills of credit and international exchange, the role of gold has become increasingly obscure, difficult for the layman to understand and, indeed, open to different interpretations by monetary specialists.

While gold has played an important part in the British monetary system for over two centuries, the international gold standard is not, as is often mistakenly supposed, a hoary institu-

[1] *Cf.* my article in the *Yale Review*, June, 1940.

tion. Generally adopted in western countries in the 1870's, it had a somewhat checkered career before World War I forced a well-nigh general abandonment. Reconstructed on modified lines in the middle of the 1920's, it was unable to survive the great depression. Country after country, through the decade of the 1930's, abandoned the gold standard, until now virtually the whole world outside the United States is on a paper basis and even in the United States gold cannot be obtained except for industrial uses and for external payments. Yet despite this fact, the output of gold increased from 22 million ounces in 1932 to about 35 million ounces in 1939.

Already in World War I, an international gold problem was created in the form of a "maldistribution of gold." By reason of the Allied demand for goods, the United States then acquired a greatly increased share in the world's monetary gold. In 1913, the United States held 27 per cent of the total monetary gold stock; in 1926, 44 per cent; in 1944, 60 per cent.

From the standpoint of the gold problem, the countries of the world may be divided into four groups. First, there are the six leading gold-holding countries, the United States, England, France, Belgium, Holland and Switzerland. These held, in 1939, 83 per cent of the world's gold reserves. Second, there are the three enemy countries, Germany, Italy (until recently) and Japan, largely denuded of their gold reserves. Third, there are the 40-odd countries which rely increasingly upon their foreign-exchange assets in the large gold-holding countries; and fourth, Russia with growing holdings.

With $21 billion worth of gold, the United States holds at present over 60 per cent of the world's monetary stocks. We acquired this vast hoard in the following manner. On January 1, 1934, just prior to our revaluation of the dollar, our gold holdings in terms of old gold dollars amounted to $4 billion. The revaluation added overnight $2.8 billion, bringing the total to $6.8 billion. During the six-year period from 1934 to 1939 inclusive, about $11 billion were purchased at home and abroad —$1 billion coming from domestic production and the compulsory return of gold coin, and $10 billion from gold imports. From 1939 to 1942 another $5 billion came in. Since 1942 we have lost about $1.7 billion in gold exports, leaving us currently (1945) with $21 billion.

Of the $16 billion gold inflow from 1934 to 1942, $6 billion may be attributable to an export surplus (of which surplus 60 per cent occurred after the outbreak of war in 1939), while the remaining $10 billion are attributable either to recorded capital inflow or to unidentified transactions.

What do our vast gold holdings mean for the American economy? Have we accumulated a great stock of metal that is about to become worthless? Does this accumulation spell inevitable inflation? What is going to come out of the new gold situation? Has the purchase of gold by the United States Treasury constituted a serious burden and a heavy cost? Standing ready to buy gold at $35 an ounce, is the United States acting the part of Santa Claus to those countries that either produce gold in large volume or own large stocks of gold? And if this is not true, is the United States, on the contrary, a bull in the international china shop, wrecking the world's monetary system?—or, to change the figure, a gigantic leech, sucking the lifeblood out of foreign countries? Some critics appear to find it difficult to make up their minds whether to regard the United States as an extravagant international benefactor or as an international villain.

Clearly, the world is undergoing a major revolution in its monetary system. The spectacular monetary events of the last quarter century, and those currently happening, have changed and are changing drastically the role of gold. These events fall logically into three periods: first, the years from 1913 to 1926; second, the nearly equal interval from 1926 to the Munich crisis in 1938; and, finally, the momentous times since that crisis.

It might be asked why I have taken the year 1926 as the end of the first period and the beginning of the second. This is because the European currencies, which had been on a fluctuating basis during World War I, had by 1926 again become stabilized. Country after country had returned to gold on a fixed basis. Though France did not formally return to gold until 1928, she had stabilized on a *de facto* basis two years earlier. Thus the year 1926 marks the end of the vagaries of World War I currencies and the beginning of the new period of stabilization.

Let us consider in particular the developments, in these periods, in the six leading gold-holding countries—the United States, England, France, Belgium, Holland and Switzerland. During that time, these six countries together accumulated an ever increasing proportion of the world's monetary gold. In 1913 they held 47 per cent of the world's gold; in 1926, 64 per cent; in 1938, 78 per cent; and in 1939, 83 per cent. It should be noted that the agricultural countries have learned to rely increasingly on their foreign-exchange holdings in these leading financial countries, and relatively less on their own gold holdings. Russia is included in these calculations.

In the period from 1913 to 1926, a moderate but not drastic shift occurred in the relative gold holdings of the United States compared with the other five countries. In 1913 the United States held 27 per cent of the world's monetary gold, while the other five large gold-holding countries held 20 per cent. In 1926 the United States held 44 per cent, while the five countries held 19 per cent. Thus the impact of World War I had caused a shift of holdings from the five countries, and notably France, to the United States.

It was argued by some authorities (and not without consider-

able justification) that the increase in the American gold holdings in this period, from 1913 to 1926, represented on the
monetary side a more or less parallel development with the
greatly increased role of the United States in the world
economy. While I do not think it is possible to argue that there
were no abnormalities in the relative holdings of the six
countries in 1926, it is, I think, nevertheless true that the distribution among these six countries was then not seriously out
of balance. It is, therefore, of special interest to observe the
relative change in the gold holdings of these six countries in
the next period, from 1926 until the Munich crisis.

A striking fact, and one that has not, I think, been generally
recognized, is that in this period the five major European gold-
holding countries together increased their gold holdings more
rapidly than did the United States. From 1926 to 1938, the
American gold holdings increased by 100 per cent, while the
gold holdings of the other five countries increased 190 per cent.
This statement I am sure will come as a surprise to most people.
It is, however, a fact that from 1926 to the time of the Munich
crisis the American percentage of increase in gold holdings was
materially smaller than the increase of the gold holdings of
England, France, Belgium, Holland and Switzerland combined.
Roughly, the American holdings had approximately doubled,
while the holdings of the five European countries had nearly
tripled in this 12-year period. These figures give us, of course,
a picture of the situation only at the beginning and at the end
of the period between 1926 and 1938.

If, however, we look into the interval between these dates,
we see that important shifts occurred in the relative holdings
of the six countries. First, there was the prodigious increase
in the French gold holdings from 1926 to 1932, with a sub-
sequent decline from 1934 on. Second, there was an enormous
increase in the gold holdings of Britain from 1933 to the time
of the Munich crisis. France made a great gain in her holdings

in the first half of the period and lost, relative to the other five countries, in the last half. Britain, on the other hand, lost relatively in the first half and gained with extraordinary rapidity in the last half. The United States lost moderately in the first half of the period, relative to the other five countries, and gained rapidly, though less rapidly than Britain, in the last half. But disregarding the shifts within the interval in question, at the end—the time of the Munich crisis—our own gold stocks were twice our holdings in 1926; France also owned twice the amount she had held in 1926; English holdings were 3.4 times greater than in 1926; Belgian holdings, 3.6 times greater; Dutch holdings, 3.6 times greater; Swiss holdings, 4.5 times greater.

The Munich crisis marked a sharp turning point in the international gold situation. In March, 1938, the five European countries combined held gold stocks at the record high level of nearly $9 billion. After that crisis, their holdings declined; while the American holdings rose from $13.1 billion in August, 1938, to $16.6 billion in August, 1939, and to nearly $22.7 billion in 1942. This accelerated concentration was not the result of monetary or gold policy; it was a consequence of the war.

We must not, however, lose sight of the fact that the relatively larger holdings of the five European countries at the time of the Munich crisis as compared with 1926 can largely be accounted for by the enormous gains in the holdings of France, Belgium, Holland and Switzerland in the eight years from 1926 to 1934. In that interval, the United States absorbed no gold whatever. But after January, 1934, the United States began to absorb gold and was rapidly catching up with the five European countries combined (relative to the 1926 holdings) when the Munich crisis broke.

It is generally admitted that this gold inflow was associated mainly with a movement of capital into the United States. It is true that from 1934 to 1939 inclusive, $2.2 billion worth of the gold inflow can be accounted for by an excess of merchandise and service "exports." But $1.8 billion worth of this amount came in the years 1938 and 1939, years in which our merchandise balance was greatly affected by our own depression and by the European rearmament demand. Thus for the most part it was capital, not goods, that offset the gold inflow.

The plain fact is that in view of the international crisis people preferred to hold assets in the United States rather than in foreign countries. Thus capital poured in. The demand for dollars created by this capital movement would have appreciated the dollar in terms of foreign currencies if gold had not filled the gap. Thus the gold movement followed the capital movement.

In the early part of the period from 1934 to 1939, Americans converted foreign assets, acquired after the United States abandoned the gold standard in April, 1933, back into dollars. The return of American capital accounts for nearly $2 billion worth of the total. But more important was the desire of foreigners, mostly European, to acquire American assets. In part, this was due to the belief that large capital gains could be made in American securities and real estate. Security and real-estate values had fallen to unprecedentedly low levels owing to the severity of the depression in the United States. Expectation of even a moderate recovery induced heavy foreign purchases of American securities. The United States appeared then to be a bargain counter for European investors. And altogether aside from price considerations, the disturbed international situation in Europe induced many foreigners to transfer assets to the United States. Capital was seeking safety and security.

It is true that had we refused to take the gold the capital inflow would have forced an appreciation of the dollar. And a sharp appreciation of the dollar would certainly have induced a severe deflation of our agricultural and raw-material prices and caused a serious depressional influence on the American economy. With security and property values thereby deflated, some considerable check could have been exerted on further capital inflow, but an equilibrium in our balance of payments achieved in this manner would have been rather costly. So long as the disequilibrium in our balance of payments was caused by such quite extraordinary factors as those that account for the capital movements to the United States, it would have been folly to rectify the disequilibrium by a sharply deflationary monetary policy. Neither the United States nor Britain was willing (and I think they were right) to deflate the internal economy sufficiently to prevent gold imports.

Some economists have argued that the gold imports constituted a heavy burden, a serious cost. All of them, of course, admit that the gold imports were not a cost for the Treasury—though this is probably not quite understood by the general public. When the man in the street reads that the government is buying gold, he may naturally think that the government thereby incurs an expense that must be covered by loans or by taxation. He does not always realize that the Treasury merely monetizes the gold that comes in. The process is in effect no different from the familiar one under the old gold standard. Then the Treasury stood ready to coin into dollars any amount of gold brought to the mint. Similarly in the recent period, the Treasury issued gold certificates (or rather gold-certificate credits), against the gold purchases, to the Federal Reserve Banks, and with the deposit account thus acquired paid for this gold. The importer who had sold the gold to the Treasury received a check which he deposited at his bank, and so demand deposits—our chief medium of exchange in modern times—were increased. The bank, in turn, deposited this check with the Federal Reserve Bank, and so member-bank reserves were increased. Thus the imported gold was monetized, and through the process of monetization the gold purchases cost the Treasury not a cent.

When some economists say, therefore, that our gold imports

constitute a heavy cost, they mean something quite different from cost to the Treasury. Such imports constitute a cost, if at all, in the sense that a foreigner can use his dollar assets, which he has acquired by means of the gold he has sent us, to buy American products. If he does, American productive resources are used to supply exported goods to foreigners, instead of to supply goods to the United States.

The businessman favors these exports. He receives payment in dollars. The wage earner is glad of them because they mean a chance to get more work and full-time earnings. He does not see anything to worry about. Economists, however, are likely to insist that we ought not to export unless we take goods and services in exchange that are useful to us and from which we can derive real utility. This idea leaves the practical business-man cold. He merely welcomes more business.

In the history of economic thought, the economics of the businessman has not infrequently been superior to that of the theorist. The economist is usually quite right if you grant his assumptions, but often his assumptions are quite unrealistic. In this particular case, the economist would be quite right if we lived in a world in which the economic system were always operating at full employment. When we have full employment, we want more imports, not more exports. But if we have large unused productive resources, the instinct of the practical businessman who welcomes exports is sound: the real income of the people of the United States is increased by an expansion of exports. This is true because the increased exports become the means through which purchasing power is distributed. In-creased employment results in increased purchases of consump-tion goods. The domestic consumption-goods industries are thereby stimulated. Moreover, the expansion of the export industries, together with the consequent stimulus to the consumption-goods industries, induces an expansion in the capital-goods industries—in plant and equipment. Thus industry in general is stimulated, the real income of the community rises and the standard of living is lifted. The economist would be quite correct if he could assume full employment without the added stimulus of exports. But this assumption is, in fact, not valid. The practical businessman is on sound ground—he is realistic. The extra exports are not a real cost, and they do not lower our standard of living. They stimulate our economy and raise the real income of the country as a whole.

Thus the superficial statement that we are poorer by $14 billion by reason of our gold imports is not very realistic. Let us, however, make the following assumptions: first, that the assets acquired by foreigners through the gold we import from them are sold and the dollar balances thus acquired are used to buy American exports; second, that these exports occur in a period in which full employment would have been achieved without the stimulus of the extra exports. Under those conditions, we should then suffer a real cost, namely, the cost of using our labor resources to supply goods to foreigners that we might otherwise have consumed ourselves. But we know from past history that we do not often have even reasonably full employment. And if we did, the real cost of any possible excess exports could scarcely ever be more than, say, 2 or 3 per cent of our total income. Enjoying full employment, no sector of the country is likely to feel any burden. Thus the conclusion with respect to cost stands or falls on the validity of the assumption made with respect to full employment.

It will be argued, however, that, in the event that foreigners acquire securities and not goods for export, the transfer of several billions of dollars' worth of American income-yielding assets to foreigners entails a loss of interest and dividends to Americans. If foreigners use the interest and dividend receipts from such securities to buy goods, we are then again thrown back on the question whether such exports are to be welcomed as a stimulus or deprecated as a burden. Again the question must be settled by reference to the amount of unemployment. More-over, the withdrawal of interest and dividends (or principal) might wholly or in part, depending on the prevailing conditions of our international account, take the form of gold exports or at least a reduction of gold imports.

It might, of course, be argued that instead of exporting to foreigners we ought to find other ways of achieving full em-ployment. For example, we might develop an adequate program of public improvement and development projects. With this I wholeheartedly agree. But we know that such a program is not always politically feasible to the extent desired. Almost all pro-posals to achieve full employment encounter serious obstacles in their practical realization. The task is difficult enough at best, and it is at any rate minimized by an export surplus. To con-tinue such a surplus, paid in gold, is indeed a confession that we have failed to solve our domestic problem. We should not be satisfied until we have solved it. In the meantime we should not confuse our thinking by alarmist assertions about the cost of gold imports.

But do not our vast gold holdings constitute an inflation threat? I do not think so. The mere fact that we have large gold reserves in no way leaves us with less control over money and prices than countries with small gold reserves, or countries like Britain operating on a managed-paper basis. If we fail to realize that despite our gold reserves we are nevertheless in fact living on a managed-currency basis, then we are in real danger. But it is reasonable, I think, to hope that no administration could, in view of recent monetary developments in theory and practice, be so unenlightened as not to realize this fact.

The gold imports did produce one very beneficial result. It produced a condition of high liquidity in our banking system and in the community as a whole. It directly increased (a) the money supply (demand deposits) and (b) excess bank reserves. Excess reserves, in turn, induced banks to increase their investments which further increased demand deposits. Without this liquidity we could not have achieved a low rate of interest. A low rate of interest has been important as a means of stimulating home building under the F.H.A. and in other investment areas. This low rate of interest we are determined to maintain.

Governor Towers has well stated the case for the maintenance of a low interest rate in the following excerpt taken from the 1944 report of the Bank of Canada:

A policy aimed at higher interest rates would only become intelligible if, after war shortages are over, consumers' expenditure and capital development were to proceed at a rate which would overstrain our productive capacity. I see no prospect of such a situation arising in a form which would call for a policy of raising interest rates. Admittedly, the rate of interest is only one of many factors influencing Canada's economic position, and it is probably not as important an instrument of control as was once supposed. It remains true, however, that the prospect of unstable interest rates could make it exceedingly difficult for business to formulate long-term plans. Moreover, high borrowing costs would hamper new investment in plant, equipment and housing, would restrict the expansion of employment, and would seriously complicate the task of government financing. There can be little doubt that the easy money policy which has been pursued since 1935 assisted in promoting recovery from the depression and facilitated the adjustments which have been required during the war period. Indication that the Bank intends to continue this easy money policy should be helpful in making plans for the future.

The high liquidity caused by the gold inflow has contributed greatly to the financing of the war at low rates of interest. The large gold reserves held by the Federal Reserve Banks permitted large purchases of government obligations by the System. This, in turn, supplied the commercial banks with adequate reserves enabling them to finance at low rates the new government issues not purchased by the public. While the last war was financed on a 4.5 per cent interest rate, this war is being financed on a 2 per cent rate.

It is, of course, true that we could have created all this liquidity both for peace and for war even though we had received no gold imports. But would we? Is it at all probable that the monetary authorities would have increased Federal Reserve credit by $14 billion had there been no gold imports? Is it probable that Congress would have lowered the legal Reserve ratio to a point that would have permitted such expansion? I doubt it. We won the high liquidity and the ensuing low interest rate through the happy accident of the gold inflow. We were therefore spared the painful process of consciously adopting a bold new policy.

Nevertheless, we cannot escape facing the issue of internal gold cover for our money supply. The war expansion is steadily reducing the Federal Reserve ratio. While the ratio may not reach the legal limit at the war's end, there will be no wide margin, if any, to spare. Accordingly, nearly all the gold stock of $21 billion will be tied up as cover for our domestic money supply. It will not be free gold available for international payments. Despite our vast gold holdings we shall not be able to afford any loss of gold. We shall not be able to use our gold to settle our accounts should our imports exceed our exports.

This is obviously a ludicrous situation. Midas has tied himself hand and foot so that he can buy nothing with his gold. We have made ourselves, unless we liberalize our regulations, perpetual gold hoarders by edict of law. I do not think we shall prove to be that foolish. We are less bound today by monetary and gold prejudices, let us hope, than we were a decade ago. While there is no immediate occasion for changing the Federal Reserve ratio, it would be wise policy to reduce it at an early date to, say, 10 per cent. Such action would free most of our gold for international payment if needed, and at the same time give the Board of Governors ample powers to stabilize the long-term rate of interest at approximately its present low level.

At the end of the war we shall hold, say, about $21 billion worth of gold while the rest of the world will hold about $14 billion. Foreign holdings will be nearly triple their stock of monetary gold in 1926. But this does not necessarily mean much. In the meantime output and income have grown enormously everywhere. More gold is needed to protect the balance of payments of many countries. Moreover, the gold is very unevenly distributed.

Nevertheless, we start off, after the war, with large gold holdings not only in the United States but elsewhere. Moreover gold production will add about $1.2 billion worth of new gold each year. Thus if the United States could achieve a balance in its international accounts, thereby stopping further gold inflows into this country, in a single decade the rest of the world would hold more gold than the United States.

It is evident, by the agreement reached at Bretton Woods, that there is no thought of demonetizing gold. Gold, as we have seen, plays an important part in the International Monetary Fund. Countries continue to rely mainly on their gold holdings to cushion gaps in their balance of payment positions. The line of credit accorded each country in the Fund is regarded merely as a supplement. We have not yet reached the point of world economic solidarity at which international credit is regarded as sufficiently secure to dispense with gold payments. Until this time is reached, gold will continue to play an important role in international monetary arrangements.

CHAPTER XVIII

INTERNATIONAL LOANS AND INVESTMENTS

WE MAY take it for granted that we do not wish to continue gold imports ad infinitum. How, then, do we solve our dilemma? We wish to export more than we import, but how do we get paid? Direct gifts, however humanitarian from a broadly cosmopolitan point of view, are politically impossible, and veiled or concealed gifts once seen through are amusing but impracticable. What about international loans? Must they inevitably wind up in default and therefore in unexpected and involuntary gifts? Must they of necessity create distortions and disequilibrium in the international economy?

These unhappy results did, indeed, in large part prevail with respect to the international loans of the interwar period. But there are several things that may be said about this episode. The foreign loans of the twenties in large part reflected the wild speculative temper of the twenties. The middlemen's profits in marketing the bonds to unsuspecting and credulous investors were not infrequently the primary purpose of the loans. Time and again the loans were made without reference to their economic validity in terms of the uses to which the funds were to be put. The rate of interest was often exorbitant and there were little or no provisions for amortization. If the funds were not used for productive purposes the borrower was in no position to make good on the debt and, moreover, the exorbitant interest rate invited default. The validity of international lending ought not to be judged on the basis of this experience.

With respect to the argument that the impact of international lending upon the world economy must inevitably cause disequilibrium and collapse, again several things need to be said. These consequences are not inevitable. For one thing foreign lending ought to be conducted on a stable basis. At the close of the twenties the vast flow of foreign lending suddenly ceased. Violent fluctuations in capital movements cannot fail to have a disrupting international effect. Foreign lending, if it is to be safe, must be controlled and managed so as to promote international stability; it must not be allowed to cause chaotic and violent fluctuations in international accounts.

Moreover, it should be pointed out that the breakdown of the exchanges after 1929 could not be charged to the burden of servicing the long-term debt. The breakdown was due to the sudden cessation of capital movements and to the rapidly cumulating world depression which created unmanageable gaps in the balance of payment position of the primary-producing and borrowing countries.

Countries can make good on their debt service charges in a stable and prosperous world with an expanding and sustained volume of world trade. They cannot do so in one that suffers such violent fluctuations as we had in the interwar period.

International lending and international investment can be managed in a way to promote (a) high levels of employment and production in the great industrial countries, (b) rising living standards and productivity in the borrowing countries and (c) world-wide economic stability. But the effect of foreign lending may well be disastrous if we rely upon automatic forces. A powerful engine will drive us into the ditch if we do not keep our hand on the throttle and on the steering wheel.

There is every reason why a large volume of international investment and international lending should be undertaken in the next decade or two. From our standpoint international lending affords an outlet for our vast volume of savings. In good years our gross savings, including depreciation and other reserves as well as net savings, are around 20 per cent of our national income—in other words, at $140 billion national income, around $28 billion. It will not be easy to find satisfactory and profitable private-investment outlets for this vast volume of savings within the territory of the United States. Foreign loans and foreign investments can make a contribution to the solution of our savings-investment problem.

On the side of the borrowing countries, they are seriously in need of capital. They could, to be sure, as did Russia in the interwar period, tighten their belts and lower their consumption standards in order to squeeze out of a low national income funds for capital development. But Russia is a totalitarian state. In general, the industrially backward countries with their freer economic system would find this process not only grievously painful but also politically impossible. Foreign loans would greatly ease their problem.

These countries need capital for the development of railroads, roads, port facilities, electric power and large-scale agricultural projects. On the basis of these developmental projects, agricultural diversification, improved agricultural techniques and industrialization up to a certain point consistent with the resources of the country become feasible. In this manner the productivity, income and purchasing power of these industrially backward countries can be raised. The increase in income and purchasing power will, in turn, reflect itself in a demand for the products which are most in demand in modern, high-standard countries and which the United States is in a peculiarly favorable condition to supply. These include automobiles, electrical appliances, radios, telephones, typewriters and the like. There need be no fear that industrialization of these countries would reduce their trade with the United States and other countries. The multiplicity and variety of products that are demanded as standards of living rise insure a rising volume of trade as these countries advance from lower to higher levels of productivity and purchasing power.

If international loans are undertaken and international investments are managed and controlled so as to insure a reasonably stable flow of capital and if the funds are invested in productive projects, we need not take a pessimistic view with respect to the possibility of repayment. Repayment obviously cannot be made if the foreign exchanges are going to be periodically disrupted by violent fluctuations in capital movements. And particularly they become impossible if the United States continues to experience violent booms and depressions. We do not know how well we shall succeed in maintaining economic stability and full employment in the United States, but it would not be sensible to refrain from a sound program of international lending merely because we are not sure how well we shall manage our own affairs. We must undertake reasonable risks. If we manage our own affairs reasonably well, if we enter into international co-operation on international monetary and financial arrangements, and if the foreign loans are invested in productive and useful projects, then it is reasonable to suppose that over a long-run period the interest and amortization charges can be paid. They will be relatively small in proportion to total international transactions and can quite easily be managed in a reasonably stable and prosperous world. It is only in terms of a rounded view of the whole problem—domestic and international—that a solution can be found. An integrated domestic and international program of expansion and trade would create the conditions under which foreign loans can be serviced and repaid.

CHAPTER XIX

IMPORTS IN A FULL-EMPLOYMENT ECONOMY

THE classical economist and the practical businessman for 100 years have taken completely divergent positions with respect to the relative economic importance of exports and imports.

The classical economist looked upon exports as a necessary evil while imports were regarded as highly desirable. Imports, he argued, added to our total flow of goods and services and increased our standard of consumption. Exports used up valuable productive resources and constituted a social cost. To be sure, this cost had to be endured in order to obtain the means with which to pay for imports. In a rational world, we export because we want imports of raw materials we do not possess or goods we cannot cheaply produce.

The practical businessman, on the other hand, was disposed to view imports critically and to favor the highest possible volume of exports. Imports competed with domestic industry and created unemployment. Exports, on the other hand, provided outlets for surplus products without saturating unduly the domestic market. Exports were desirable ends in themselves and were to be welcomed.

These conflicting views were never satisfactorily reconciled. The practical businessman viewed the economist's analysis with distrust, if not, indeed, with contempt, and set him down as an impractical dreamer.

The practical businessman usually gained his point in terms of public policy. He was realistic and essentially right in terms of the facts of economic life that daily confronted him. The classical economist made his analysis on the assumption, not always explicitly stated, of full employment. But this condition was rarely fulfilled in a world experiencing, except at periodic boom intervals, unemployment and unused resources. The classical economist's emphasis on imports and his disdain of exports just did not fit the facts.

Reliance upon the automatic factors did not produce sustained full employment as assumed by the classical economist. Modern fiscal policy, including a compensatory tax and expenditure program, an adequate program of social security, a long-range developmental program and other measures such as an expansionist pricing policy, can, it is increasingly believed, achieve reasonably well what could not be attained by exclusive reliance on automatic forces. Thus fiscal policy with its emphasis on full employment comes to the support of classical doctrine. If full employment can by these means be achieved, then the classical analysis with respect to the importance of imports becomes realistic and for the first time can make an appeal to practical men of affairs.

If we can achieve through a compensatory and developmental fiscal program adequate markets for all we are able to produce, then we need no longer have any fear of imports. So long as imports tend to create unemployment, we cannot expect them to be welcomed by businessmen and wage earners seeking jobs. When businessmen, however, are confronted with good markets for their products and jobs are available to all who seek work, then it will be clear to everyone that goods imported from abroad are a net gain to our real income and our consumption standards. If we have engaged for many decades past in international lending and if in consequence we are receiving imports from other countries as payment for the interest and amortization charges, these imports will in a full-employment society be welcomed. Not only can we enjoy the goods and services that we are able to produce at home but in addition the excess of imports over exports due us as a creditor country. Thus our real income would be raised over and above our current production by our capacity to draw on income from foreign investments. Here is the realistic reconciliation between the classical economist and the practical businessman.

In a world in which full employment is reasonably well maintained all around we shall be able to come much closer to an optimum international division of labor than we have ever attained in the past. In such a world it becomes blatantly foolish to waste productive resources on products that can be far more economically imported from abroad. In a full-employment society it will be much easier to reduce tariff barriers and remove quantitative restrictions on imports. In a full-employment society subsidization of exports, whether directly or by currency depreciation, will not be tolerated. In a full-employment society emphasis will be placed not upon exports but upon imports.

CHAPTER XX

THE UNITED STATES' STAKE IN THE STERLING-BLOCKED BALANCES

Two drastic changes have occurred which will affect the post-war trade position of the United Kingdom. The first is the loss of a considerable income from foreign investments and from shipping and other services. This will affect its ability to import and, accordingly, our export trade to Britain. The second is the accumulation of blocked sterling balances by India, the Dominions, and other members of the sterling area. This will affect our exports to many parts of the empire and to countries closely related by economic ties.

It is evident that the international position of Great Britain has deteriorated very seriously under the impact of World War II. Great Britain will have changed from the position of a creditor country to that of a debtor country. Formerly the United Kingdom was able to finance a surplus of imports over exports from income earned on foreign investments, shipping receipts, and income from insurance and other services. These earnings from all parts of the world will be greatly reduced.

At the outbreak of the war, British investments in the United States amounted to about $2 billion. Prior to the lend-lease agreement, Great Britain was compelled to purchase large quantities from the United States. This was paid for partly by gold shipments and partly by the sale of American securities held in England. By 1941 about $500 million worth of such securities were liquidated. In addition, another $500 million worth of securities were placed as collateral with the New York Federal Reserve Bank as trustee for a loan to Britain by the Reconstruction Finance Corporation.[1] Thus one-half of the dollar exchange formerly available from British investments in the United States is lost.

Total British foreign assets in 1939 amounted to about $16 billion, which in good times earned about $0.8 billion. These assets have been heavily deflated in consequence of the war. Besides the liquidation of American securities, various parts of the empire have repurchased their own securities held in Britain, the proceeds being used by the United Kingdom to buy needed commodities and matériel for war. In addition, the Dominions and other parts of the empire have accumulated large sterling balances in London in exchange for war exports.

[1] Cf. *Some Factors in Postwar Export Trade with the British Empire*, Economic Series No. 39, Bureau of Foreign and Domestic Commerce, September, 1944.

By the end of 1944 it is estimated that sterling balances, representing short-term indebtedness by Britain mainly to the empire, amounted to nearly $12 billion.

Thus England comes out of the war with her foreign assets drastically reduced and with short-term debts more than offsetting her remaining long-term assets. From a creditor country with $16 billion worth of foreign assets earning about $0.8 billion income a year, she will emerge from the war a debtor country.

The repatriation of securities held in England, especially by India, Canada and South Africa, represents a severe loss of foreign exchange for Britain. But this shift represents a gain in the foreign-exchange position of important parts of the empire. Since, however, these empire countries now have large accumulated balances in London, the question arises: How free are they, or will they be, to use their foreign-exchange resources to buy goods in the United States? Will not the accumulated sterling balances, in one way or another, compel or induce them to use these balances to pay for goods purchased in England?

The members of the sterling area are required under current arrangements to turn over any free foreign exchange that they may acquire in trade with other countries to the Foreign Exchange Pool operated by the Bank of England for the British Treasury. In return for delivering such exchange to the Pool, these countries receive a balance in sterling. Thus the members of the sterling area accumulate sterling balances not only from their large war exports to Britain but also from excess exports to other countries, notably the United States. These blocked sterling balances are held in the form of demand deposits, short-term Treasury bills, and other government securities.

Member countries in the sterling area can trade freely with each other within the limits of wartime regulations with respect to allocation of materials, shipping and the like. But countries in the sterling area may not import from outside countries except by application for an import permit. If the import permit is granted, application is made for foreign exchange with which to pay for the imports, and this is usually granted automatically. Exports to countries outside the sterling area are permitted only if payment is made in a foreign currency. This insures that exports will contribute to the supply of foreign exchange needed for war purchases. If exports do not so contribute, they would be regarded as a misuse of manpower at a time when all resources are needed for the war effort and would therefore rightly be prohibited.

The Indian sterling balances, by far the largest, have arisen largely from exports to England and, in part, from dollar exchange resulting from American military expenditures in that area. The dollar exchange thus obtained was turned over to the Foreign Exchange Pool of the Bank of England in exchange for sterling balances. It would be in the interest of the Indian government if the dollars arising from military expenditures in that area could be earmarked for India's postwar use. Similarly, American loans to India, freed from the sterling-pool arrangement, would enable India to import goods from this country. Until the system of sterling-area control of foreign exchange is liberalized, trade between the United States and various parts of the empire will necessarily be on a restricted basis.

During the transition period, comprising some years following the end of hostilities, exchange control and other means of controlling imports will be continued in greater or less degree. If exchange is short, it will have to be used to satisfy the most essential needs first. And the sterling-blocked balances will at best remain to plague us. Anything approaching multilateral trade will not be possible until these short-term debts are funded into long-term debts with specific provision for gradual repayment over several decades. But even so, the only way England can pay off these debts is to expand her exports in excess of the exports required to balance her normal current requirements. This means that the countries having sterling balances, if they expect to take payment, will have to buy British goods in greater volume than they would under the normal conditions of multilateral trade. This is the situation confronting us in our trade relations with the British Empire.

Part of the sterling-blocked balances may be scaled down by lend-lease or mutual-aid agreement between Britain and her creditors. This appears to be possible in view of the fact that they originated largely in consequence of the war effort. For the rest, long-term financing arrangements will likely constitute an important method of settlement. Such financing arrangements might well provide for a further reduction in the debt in exchange for long-term interest rates somewhat higher than the very low rates now paid on the current balances. Thus in one way or another, it may be expected that the debt would be substantially reduced.

The replacement of the current short-term debt by a long-term debt would permit a gradual repayment over a long period, perhaps 40 or 50 years. While this would greatly minimize the problem, there would nevertheless remain from such a settlement a considerable influence upon the future direction and distribution of world trade.

Not all of the sterling balances can be regarded as abnormal. The empire countries usually hold large sterling balances partly as reserve for their internal currency circulation and partly as ordinary working balances for current trade. Prior to the war, the central banks throughout the empire held around $1 billion in the form of sterling balances for monetary reserves and for working trade balances. At the end of the war they are likely to hold much larger reserves. Thus in a free-exchange market, a not inconsiderable part of the sterling balances will be desired for monetary reserves and working trade balances. This minimizes in some measure the problem.

The suggestion has been made that the sterling balance might be funded into a long-term debt and sold to the United States. While this would permit an early freeing of sterling exchange (as would, also, the funding arrangement with her present creditors as discussed above) the solution is far from a happy one. It is not easy to see how international equilibrium is improved by transforming Britain's debt to the empire into one to the United States. After the last war we became a long-term creditor of England and the result was very unhappy indeed. We are not likely to wish to repeat this experience. The immediate effect of such a long-term debt would be to create a heavy demand for dollars in order to service the amortization and interest charges. But there is already likely to be a shortage of dollars. It would seem wiser for Britain to fund the debt to her present creditors and for the United States to contribute in other ways to a solution along lines that will serve our own long-run interests and at the same time promote world-wide trade.

The shift of the United Kingdom from a creditor to a debtor country will profoundly influence its ability to import. Before the war, the excess of British imports over exports (nearly $1.6 billion) was financed from the earnings from overseas investments (about $0.8 billion) and from shipping, insurance and other services. All these sources of foreign exchange have diminished, the decline being estimated at around $500 million.

How, then, can Britain balance her international account? She may reduce her imports or increase her exports. In 1913 the ratio of British imports to the national income was 35 per cent. By 1938 the ratio of imports to income had fallen to 21 per cent. Whether or not this trend may continue depends fundamentally upon world developments.

British economists have estimated that England must increase her exports by 50 per cent over her prewar exports in order to pay for necessary imports and to offset the loss of foreign exchange owing to the liquidation of foreign investments and the decline in earnings from services of various kinds and also to pay off gradually the frozen sterling balances. So large an increase in exports would require larger imports of raw materials. Thus any gain in exports is not all net. It will therefore be difficult to provide a requisite volume of exports to balance Britain's international account.

It would be to our advantage to promote, by means of international collaboration on many fronts, a high level of world prosperity and world trade so that England may balance her accounts by increasing her exports. To the extent that this is made possible, she will not be compelled to pursue restrictive measures on her imports—measures that would be seriously damaging to our own foreign trade.

CHAPTER XXI

MONOPOLY AND INTERNATIONAL CARTELS

BROADLY speaking there are two points of view with respect to cartels. According to one view, international cartels should be completely suppressed and eliminated. They should be destroyed, root and branch, by the concerted action of leading countries. If this is impossible, at any rate the United States ought rigorously to prohibit American participation. According to this point of view, cartels have no function to perform and are to be regarded per se as antisocial institutions.

According to another point of view, cartels have arisen in consequence of modern economic conditions. They cannot arbitrarily be uprooted since they are a means of accommodation and adjustment to deep-seated problems that cannot easily be brushed aside. Cartels may indeed as they have operated in the past have had unfortunate economic consequences, but this does not necessarily imply that their structure, organization and functions may not be so adjusted as to perform a useful purpose.

These opposing points of view in respect to international cartels are not unlike the opposing points of view with respect to trade unions. To be sure, relatively few economists today take the position that trade unions are inherently bad and ought to be eliminated. Formerly a large section of economic opinion favored this view and it still persists in certain quarters. Increasingly the view has won ground that trade unionism is a necessary institution under modern conditions, that its abuses must be eliminated as far as possible and that its organization and procedure must be adapted so as to serve the useful purpose of promoting good labor relations, fostering increasing productivity and a fair division of the product of industry.

That international cartels may in certain limited areas of economic life prove to be useful institutions under modern economic conditions, that their uneconomic and antisocial policies can be eliminated, and that they can be reformed and reorganized so as to promote a well-functioning economic order, is a view that is currently sharply challenged. The analogy of trade unions suggested above should certainly not be accepted lightly.

It may be observed that international industrial cartels have frequently been organized in heavy-goods industries and in certain basic mineral products. These areas are peculiarly subject to violent fluctuations in the business cycle. An industry that suffers violent fluctuations cyclically in the quantity of goods sold is inevitably cursed with excess capacity. Capacity is built up to meet the requirements of the peak load of the boom period; but speculative and excessively optimistic expectations engendered in the boom cause capacity to be built up even beyond the requirements of the peak load. It may further be observed that heavy-goods industries require a very large amount of fixed capital. Since the variable costs are relatively low, competitors are under pressure to take markets away from each other by cutthroat competition. Unless they can combine and divide the market in some manner, this process leads into bankruptcy. The process of cutthroat competition is particularly likely to occur in third-country markets where an added increment of output may be dumped to advantage at prices far below average unit cost.

With respect to international agricultural commodity agreements, again a basic problem is that of overcapacity. This overcapacity relates in part to (a) the inelasticity of demand for agricultural products and the limited growth over time in the demand for these products in relation to the ever rising demand for industrial products, (b) the continued advance in the technical efficiency of agriculture, (c) the pressure of population growth in rural areas and in primary-producing countries and (d) the overstimulation of agriculture incident to World War I and now again to World War II.

The basic problem underlying the formation of both international industrial cartels and international agricultural commodity agreements—namely, the adjustment of normal supply to normal demand—can in considerable measure be met by reducing the fluctuations of the cycle and achieving a relatively high degree of stability at full-employment income levels. With respect to international industrial cartels, if the violent cyclical fluctuations could largely be eliminated, a major cause for excess capacity (and hence the inducement to restrictive practices) would be removed. With respect to agricultural commodities it is evident that a considerable part of the excess capacity of agriculture would disappear in the event of a sustained full-employment income.

The function of international commodity agreements is fundamentally to facilitate a long-run adjustment of normal supply to normal demand without causing the painful and indeed unendurable hardships to the producers which inevitably follow from permitting an automatic adjustment to take its course. A constructive approach to the problem therefore involves not merely adjustment of production to current demand but also ways and means of finding new uses and new outlets for the product in question and of transferring the submarginal farmers to other regions and to other industries in the economy.

The function of international industrial cartels properly conceived should also be to adjust capacity to normal demand, at the same time promoting efficiency and adjusting the selling price in accordance with unit costs at reasonably full utilization of plant and equipment.

The essential evils of monopoly considered from the standpoint of their effect upon the *economic* functioning of the society can be briefly stated. They relate (*a*) to restriction and suppression of technical improvements, (*b*) to an uneconomic use of resources and (*c*) to an intensification of the savings-investment problem.

International cartels, as is well known, have been guilty of the suppression of patents. And monopoly, by charging an excessive price for the product, causes a distortion in the price structure, an uneconomic restriction in the output of the excessively priced product, and so an uneconomic use of resources. Monopoly, moreover, has the effect of yielding monopoly profits. Either the wage is too low or the price is too high.

The consumption of the masses is thereby restricted. Excessive profits feed into the flow of savings and thereby the savings-investment problem is intensified.

To deal with these problems, it may be doubted whether mere trust-busting and periodic prosecution in the courts are very effective devices. Instead—as indeed is increasingly recognized by the United States Department of Justice—a continuous administrative correction of abuses is required. This involves an administrative unit in the Department of Justice which constantly keeps itself informed of current practices and developments in the various organizations and corporations in question, and which is therefore in a position to prevent abusive practices at the source rather than to perform a major operation after the cancerous growth has developed.

Such continued administrative control requires, if it is to be adequate and effective, a far more comprehensive and detailed control of accounting procedure than has heretofore been achieved.

With respect to international cartels, an International Authority might be instituted which would continuously be on the job to prevent at the outset abusive practices. Such an International Authority, to be effective, might have to be adequately represented on the boards of international cartels, where feasible.

In order to prevent the suppression and restriction of technical improvements, a major reform in our patent system is necessary. For one thing, is there any good reason why patents as such should not be completely abolished, substituting therefor a royalty for the inventor and permitting all companies, upon paying such a royalty, free use of the new device and free opportunity to develop new techniques, new products and new processes?

The government ought, moreover, to set up a research institute amply financed which would give promising careers to able young scientists. Such a government research institute, set up on an adequate scale, could be expected to increase very greatly the number of young men undertaking graduate studies in physics, chemistry and engineering and would provide us with a far richer supply of the most important resource any country can have—scientific knowledge and scientific personnel. The results of such a government research institute should be made available freely to all companies.

With respect to the savings-investment problem, three approaches are suggested. One relates to the control of prices. Adequate accounting procedure, continuous up-to-date information on unit costs, and publicity with respect to these facts would make it difficult for a corporation to maintain arbitrarily monopolistic prices quite out of line with the cost situation. The growing strength of trade unions broadly considered can be expected to act as a restraining factor upon excessive monopoly profits. If, in fact, price control should prove inadequate and excessive monopoly profits should prevail over a considerable period, trade-union action may be expected to increase wages. Such action is socially legitimate up to a certain point, but within fairly restricted limits. Trade unions in a monopoly industry are entitled to rising wages as productivity increases and it may even be justifiable for them to set the pace for wage advances for the country as a whole. But it is not legitimate for the trade union in a monopoly industry merely to share with the owners of the industry antisocial monopoly profits.

From the broad social standpoint, in the event that price control does not prove adequate a final approach to the problem is through taxation of monopoly profits. This, however, must be regarded as a policy of last resort. While taxes might capture excessive profits, it would still be true that a monopoly price, unjustified by the cost situation, distorts the structure of prices and results in uneconomic use of resources. The only really basic approach to the problem is the continued adjustment of prices to unit costs, and hence the elimination of excessive monopoly profits.

Aside from the purely economic aspects of monopoly, there are also the political implications. Monopolistic organizations and corporations must be made the servants of a well-functioning economic and political society and not its masters. A wholesome safeguard against monopolistic political power lies in the growth of the labor movement, of the co-operative movement, and of an enlightened public opinion functioning through the power of a democratic political state. Unfortunately in this country the co-operative movement is weak and its prospects in the future are not bright. Thus we are robbed of one of the main safeguards against excessive monopoly power which some European countries enjoy. We are therefore forced to rely upon the counterbalancing power of the labor movement and upon an increasingly enlightened public opinion.

CHAPTER XXII

International Collaboration vs. Economic Isolationism

AFTER World War I the United States turned isolationist along political lines. We are now convinced that this was a great mistake. We are now prepared to go along on a world political organization designed to maintain the peace of the world. But are we prepared to back up such a peace security organization with the economic policies, international and domestic, necessary to provide the requisite economic foundation for world security?

Along economic lines two questions confront this country. First, is the United States prepared to co-operate effectively in international economic institutions such as the Bretton Woods Monetary and Financial Plans or the Dumbarton Oaks Proposal for an Economic and Social Council? And second, is the United States prepared to "pull its weight" in the world economy by maintaining full employment and a high level of income at home?

We are confronted in the program for international economic co-operation now before the Congress with a decision no less significant than that of our adherence to the League of Nations after World War I. Whatever arguments may be made with respect to details (about which there will always be differences that must of necessity be resolved by compromise) the fact is that adherence to these institutions for international economic collaboration will in large measure determine what kind of a postwar world we shall have. A world political federation is not enough. Without economic international co-operation, political arrangements are bound to fail. Having become internationalist on political lines there is the gravest danger that the United States will remain isolationist on economic lines.

There can be little question that the whole world will be watching to see which way the United States is going. And it will be quick to conclude that American collaboration along political lines is an empty gesture if economic co-operation is refused. This is the gist of the matter. We are confronted with issues that will be decisive for many generations to come. We are facing another crisis in our international relations not unlike that high-lighted in the famous Lodge-Lowell debates of 25 years ago.

But in laying our plans for a durable peace and for international security we cannot afford to overlook the threat to the stability of any international arrangements, whether political or economic, that would arise if this great country experienced a recurrence of deep depression and prolonged mass unemployment.

It is precisely the uncertainty with respect to the future of the American economy that looms up as a major disturbing element in the postwar outlook throughout the world. The impact of the United States upon world trade and world prosperity is very great. Unemployment and a low level of output in our mass-production industries have a profoundly depressing effect upon world prices. Unemployment and depression here drastically reduce American purchases of raw materials, luxury products and tourist-travel expenditures throughout the world, with repercussions back upon ourselves. Foreign countries have every reason to fear the economic impact of this country upon world affairs if we continue to have violent economic fluctuations or chronic unemployment.

Thus the whole world is eagerly watching the progress of postwar plans in the United States. World security and world peace depend in a very fundamental sense upon how good a job we do in managing our own economy. Prosperity and full employment in the United States are a basic prerequisite to world political and economic security.

It is therefore doubly tragic that we face our own future without assurance and confidence. We have as yet reached no agreement among ourselves as a nation on any dependable and far-reaching program to insure postwar full employment.

Such a program involves many things. But central and basic to all others is a compensatory and developmental program. It is encouraging to find the governors in the Missouri River Valley urging the federal government to set up a Missouri Valley Authority. Regional resource development, urban redevelopment, housing, education, public health, social security

—these are all parts of a broad developmental program designed to improve both our human and our material resources and to provide an ever rising standard of living. We need to plan now clear through the blueprint stage a $50 billion federal, state and local improvement and developmental program extending over a six- to eight-year period. In addition, this country should play its part in international investment as a means to provide outlets for our savings. Within the framework of a far-reaching developmental program—domestic and international—there will be room for sufficient flexibility so as to offset cyclical fluctuations in the private sector in the economy.

The British government has put forward a far-reaching plan for a comprehensive system of social security. Even more fundamental (since upon it depends the success of social security) is the *White Paper on Employment Policy*. This paper sets out the means whereby stable and full employment may be secured in the postwar period. Even more far reaching is *Full Employment in a Free Society* by Sir William Beveridge.

The Australian delegation at the ILO Conference at Philadelphia, and again at the Monetary and Financial Conference at Bretton Woods, urged that governments enter into an international agreement, each to maintain full employment in its own domestic economy. It was urged that domestic policies aiming at high levels of employment by expansionist measures are of international concern because of their effect upon the *demand* for goods and services. This demand is the final source of trade. The experience of the interwar period shows that the volume of international trade is highly dependent upon the level of employment in the great industrial nations. When employment and prosperity are high, trade has flourished even though hampered by tariffs and other restraints on trade. Domestic high employment and prosperity can override fairly serious obstacles to trade and have, in fact, despite these obstacles, produced a high level of international trade. Moreover, the condition of full employment is favorable for the removal of excessive barriers to world trade. Without high levels of employment and purchasing power, the real motive force behind international trade is lacking.

Domestic policies aiming at full employment are of international concern also because unless employment is maintained, other international agreements cannot function successfully. The Australian delegates urged that unless business fluctuations can be reduced, monetary and trade arrangements, however well devised, may not endure. When employment and business fall off, there inevitably ensues a struggle between countries to capture as large a share as possible of a dwindling trade. Scourged by unemployment, countries will seize upon whatever means of relief lie at hand. Unbalance in international accounts arise. Restrictive measures will be introduced. Thus import quotas, tariff abnormalities, competitive currency depreciation and bilateralism return to plague us.

An international agreement to maintain full employment does not, of course, insure that all countries will succeed in this undertaking. Each enters into the commitment in good faith, but all are aware that perfection cannot be achieved. It was fully recognized by the Australian delegates that the fear of men and women everywhere, haunted by memories of unemployment, will not be fully allayed until there is evidence over a considerable period that nations in fact are able to maintain employment. Nevertheless, it was urged that acceptance by nations of an obligation to maintain employment would do much to mobilize public opinion everywhere to see that the obligation was carried out.

Some have objected that domestic policies of employment are the sovereign concern of nations and should not be made the subject of international agreement. But the tariff of a country and the foreign-exchange value of its currency have equally been regarded as matters of sovereignty. In the final analysis, the sovereignty of a nation is not threatened when a country recognizes the unescapable fact that it lives in a world of many nations, and that its own well-being is furthered by the making of international agreements.

The Australian delegates did not suggest the creation of an international employment authority endowed with the power to interfere with the domestic policy of any country. The ways and means to secure and maintain full employment would be left to each country to determine. As we have seen in earlier chapters of this book, domestic employment may indeed be created by measures that injure other countries—measures that have been well designated by the phrase "beggar-my-neighbor" policies. But these are neither necessary nor desirable measures. Indeed, it is one of the objects of international economic co-operation to reduce such measures to a minimum. But other than these internationally undesirable measures, every country would be free to determine its own employment policies.

In some countries the state will play its role in a mixed system in which public utilities, railroads and industries that tend to become monopolistic are state owned and operated. In others, greater reliance will be placed upon private enterprise, the role of the state being largely confined to sustaining adequate total demand by means of social-security measures and developmental projects that are socially productive but not profitable for private enterprise. The conditions confronting different countries will vary, both in terms of the investment opportunities for private enterprise and in terms of the social and political climate. Yet in most modern democracies the pattern, broadly conceived, is the same. In all of these countries, private enterprise will employ a large majority of the population. In all, conditions of employment will be determined by voluntary collective bargaining with minimum conditions established by labor legislation. In all, the state will play a highly significant role in the provision of social services, including education, health, housing for low-income groups and social security; and in the provision of community and regional improvement and development projects, including standard public works, transportation facilities, agricultural development projects, urban redevelopment, the control and development of river and water resources and the development and conservation of natural resources. These things are basic to all modern democracies. And in all the industrial countries, public expenditures by now play so large a role in income formation that fiscal policy of necessity has become a major instrument of control and an important means to maintain high and stable employment.

An international commitment by all countries to maintain high levels of domestic employment would contribute greatly to the success and workability of all other international economic arrangements. These economic arrangements, in turn, are necessary and basic foundations upon which to build world political security. The various plans that have already been established or agreed to in international conferences—relief and rehabilitation, food and agriculture, commodity stabilization agreements, labor conditions, monetary arrangements, world reconstruction and development and, finally, the coordinating and integrating Economic and Social Council projected at Dumbarton Oaks—these are important beginnings. More needs to be done. But we are on the way, and we must press forward until we have achieved that measure of international co-operation necessary to provide a solid economic foundation for world political security.

APPENDIX A

EXCHANGE CONTROL AND
PRIMARY-PRODUCING COUNTRIES

PERMANENT international institutions such as (*a*) an International Monetary Fund, (*b*) an International Bank for Reconstruction and Development, (*c*) an International Commodity Corporation and (*d*) an International Economic and Social Council are being designed to promote economic international stability, world prosperity, full employment in the advanced countries, higher levels of productivity in the backward countries and a high level of world trade.

These goals, it is now generally agreed, cannot be realized by reversion to international laissez faire. A mere reliance on the automatic functioning of the price system will not accomplish these ends. Indeed, it is because this is by now widely recognized that international institutions such as those indicated above are now being planned.

We can no longer hope to achieve international equilibrium by merely relying on the automatic functioning of the gold standard. But if we set the gold standard aside, something else must take its place, or else chaotic conditions will derive from competitive exchange depreciation. The International Monetary Fund is designed on the one side to achieve reasonable exchange stability and on the other to provide reasonable flexibility. Thus this proposed international institution is expected not to prohibit exchange depreciation but to regularize the process of exchange adjustment.

Likewise, it is increasingly recognized that the legitimate goals of the undeveloped countries cannot be achieved by reliance on the old ideologies, which had nothing to contribute as a positive solution except the maintenance of a free price and exchange market. If the older ideologies prevail, the backward countries can be expected to continue to remain very largely economic colonies.

The primary-producing countries need above all (a) diversification of agriculture, (b) a moderate degree of industrialization consistent with their resources, especially the manufacture of light consumers' goods, and (c) basic developmental projects, including improved transportation, electric power development and other projects. These things will not automatically happen under the functioning of a free world market. They require international planning and the continued guidance of international institutional arrangements.

To achieve the ends sought two things are necessary: (a) the export from the older countries of technical skill and guidance—scientists, agricultural technicians and engineers, and (b) export of equipment from the mature industrial countries.

Quite obviously it is impossible to achieve any rapid increase in productivity in these backward countries without a large volume (large relative to the size of these economies) of capital formation. In the period between the two wars Russia set aside approximately 30 per cent of her national income in capital formation. This is the foundation upon which Russia's great industrial and military strength now rests. The Russian planned economy, while expanding production, curtailed consumption and thus distilled out of the productive process a vast volume of capital formation.

The relatively underdeveloped countries can achieve this end by less rigorous methods and without resorting to totalitarian organization. But it is not likely that they can make any rapid progress in this direction without deliberate international planning and collaboration.

In order to obtain the capital necessary to diversify, industrialize and construct the basic developmental projects, consumption must be restrained. For the industrially underdeveloped countries this does not, however, mean necessarily an absolute reduction in the consumption of the masses. It does mean a curtailment of the high propensity to import consumers' goods especially by the upper classes. This high propensity to import must be brought under control. This is particularly true in the postwar period. If it is not brought under control, the accumulated dollar balances piled up during the war are likely to be dissipated largely in consumption imports. They ought to be conserved for needed capital formation.

If the propensity to import consumers' goods is brought under control, much of the needed capital equipment can be imported from the United States and other industrial countries and paid for out of export proceeds, thereby reducing the burden of foreign debt. This is an important consideration from the standpoint of international equilibrium.

It is very doubtful whether the high propensity to import consumers' goods can be adequately brought under control without exchange control. The International Monetary Fund ought not to take a doctrinaire view with respect to exchange control. It is not expected to take a doctrinaire view with respect to exchange adjustment. Exchange depreciation at times will be regarded not only as appropriate but even as necessary to achieve international equilibrium. Similarly, exchange control by countries in a certain stage of economic development should be regarded as not only legitimate but also necessary in order to promote world prosperity and international equilibrium.

Exchange control is, moreover, an important instrument for

stability in a country suffering violent fluctuations in its balance of payments due to (a) crop failures in major export commodities and (b) depression in foreign markets.

Multilateral trade and free exchange (instrumented through the international institutions referred to above), it is believed, can best serve international prosperity and equilibrium in a very large part of the modern world, including the British Empire, the United States and the greater part of Europe. Moreover, as the primary-producing countries gradually evolve toward a more balanced and mixed economy, they may be expected to become ripe for admission into the circle of multilateral trade and free exchange. Exchange control can, in the meantime, serve as a useful incubator in the process of growth and development.

Side by side with the process of development and capital formation, internal institutional arrangements in these backward countries should be set up to promote a larger flow of internal savings. The high propensity to consume and the thin margin of savings in these economies create a situation in which fluctuations in the money supply account in large measure for the price-volatile character of these primitive economies. It is because the consumption function impinges so closely upon the level of output that fluctuations in the money supply produce closely corresponding fluctuations in price. In these primitive countries unemployment is a relatively minor problem; inflation and price instability are a perpetual evil.

What needs to be accomplished, of course, is not to lower the level of consumption but to raise the level of output. But as this process goes on through agricultural diversification, industrialization and basic developmental projects, the margin between consumption and output should be widened so as to develop a larger flow of internal savings. This would promote internal stability and at the same time provide internal means for capital formation as the process of development moves on.

Savings institutions and facilities should be developed, including guaranteed and insured home mortgages, government savings bonds and public savings institutions.

While the industrially mature countries need to devise ways and means of raising the consumption function as a means to promote full employment, the primitive countries should promote institutional arrangements that will increase the flow of savings, on the part of those sections of the population able to save, parallel with the process of raising productivity and output.

Important parts of the program of development in the primitive countries, moreover, must consist of improvement in (a) education (both general and technical), (b) public health, and (c) nutrition. Mere emphasis upon capital formation, agricultural diversification and basic improvement projects is not enough. Simultaneously with these developments, a large investment must be made in the human resources of these countries.

APPENDIX B

A Note on "Fundamental Disequilibrium"

Professor Haberler, in his illuminating article in the *Review of Economic Statistics* for November, 1944, concludes that the term "fundamental disequilibrium" should be interpreted by means of an objective, unambiguous and observable criterion. Such a criterion, he concludes, could only be an actual deficit in the balance of payments, but he suggests that it must be left to the judgment of the managers of the Monetary Fund to decide how large the deficit must be and how long it must last before the disequilibrium can be regarded as fundamental.

I am not at all convinced that an actual deficit in the balance of payments, or its absence, is a satisfactory criterion on the basis of which to determine the presence, or absence, of a fundamental disequilibrium. My skepticism is no doubt related to the fact that I should seriously question whether in most cases a deficit in the balance of payments can in fact be cured by a change in the exchange rate. I do not deny, however, that along with other measures a change in the exchange rate may, in certain specific cases, help.

A wrong exchange rate may not reflect itself in a deficit in the balance of payments at all. As Dr. Nurkse [1] has pointed out, and as Professor Haberler has reiterated, there was no deficit in the balance of payments in England in 1925-30. Yet in the judgment of most competent students, the pound was overvalued. The overvalued pound was reflected not in a deficit in the balance of payments but in a serious deflationary pressure upon prices and wages, especially in the export industries, and in widespread unemployment. Similarly, in the period 1931-33, the depreciation of the currencies of many countries had no significant effect upon the American balance of payment position, but exerted a strong downward pressure upon American prices. American industries competing with import industries took their licking by meeting the price competition of depreciated currencies. But they held their own in the market. American imports did not rise.

The essential point, I think, is that the price elasticity of exports and imports is by and large not very great. A change in the foreign-exchange rate can affect the balance of payments only in so far as the price elasticity of exports and imports is relatively high. An incorrect exchange rate creates a disequi-

[1] Ragnar Nurkse, *International Currency Experience*, League of Nations, Princeton University Press, New Jersey, 1944.

librium not so much in the balance of payments as in the internal cost-price structure of the country in question. An overvalued currency has a deflationary effect on prices, distorts the cost-price balance and contributes to unemployment. On the other side, while an undervalued currency eases the price competition of foreign competitors, the volume of internal investment may be so low as to create internal deflation and depression despite the favorable exchange rate. Nevertheless a favorable exchange rate makes easier a program of expansion whenever such a program is undertaken by the government.

It seems to me, therefore, that there is a far greater core of truth in the "purchasing power parity" theory than either Dr. Nurkse or Professor Haberler admit. I should rather state it in terms of "cost structure parity," since admittedly the purchasing power concept is too loose and ambiguous for reasons that have been adequately discussed in the literature of the past two decades. An exchange rate may be regarded as correct if it affords no "artificial" advantage in international competition. This means that when all of the productive resources of a country are fully employed, the exchange rate shall not artificially divert certain industries to the foreign market. A correct exchange rate is one in which only those productive resources of the country are employed in exports that have a comparative advantage in the foreign markets on the basis of an economic, world-wide allocation of resources. The exchange rate of a country should be adjusted so that its cost structure will tend to be pushed neither downward nor upward by the given exchange rate. An equilibrium exchange rate is therefore one that represents a "parity" in the cost structure of the different countries.

It would probably not be very difficult to discover serious departures from an equilibrium exchange rate if all countries really enjoyed full employment. Under these conditions the "pull" of the foreign market in the case of an undervalued currency, or the price-depressant effect of foreign competitors in the case of an overvalued currency, would be fairly easy to detect. In the case, however, of varying degrees of employment in different countries and in various phases of a violently fluctuating business cycle, the cost-price-structure relationship within any one country is seriously distorted. Unit costs are abnormally high when utilization of capacity is low. Unit labor costs are high, though wage rates would in fact prove to be low if capacity were fully utilized. The distortion of the cost structure, under depression conditions, makes international comparisons difficult.

It is a question whether variation in the exchange rate should be used as a means to remedy artificial price competition from foreign countries caused by divergencies of the cycle behavior of different countries. Should such divergencies really become serious, it may be that temporary exchange control would provide a more appropriate remedy. In all events, neither short-run cyclical fluctuations in exchange rates nor the imposition of exchange control at certain phases of the cycle could give us at all a satisfactory international economy. Merely to mention such remedies only underlines and stresses the urgent necessity of co-ordination of internal policy to maintain full employment and to iron out the cycle in all important countries.

If a country is under continuous and strong price deflationary influences from the outside world, it can, I think, be concluded that its exchange rate is out of line and should be adjusted. This is a case of a fundamental disequilibrium. Such a country may, however, not be suffering a deficit in its balance of payments. In view of the way business is organized under modern conditions, the consequences of a foreign-exchange rate that is out of equilibrium may not be a deficit in the balance of payments but rather price deflation and unemployment. This is the kind of a case which, I think, will most commonly come before the Governing Board of the Monetary Fund.

In determining whether the condition of deflation and unemployment is caused, or at least intensified, by a wrong exchange rate, judgment must, of course, be applied to various
matters. The country may be depressed by reason of a low
volume of domestic investment. It should not be utterly impossible to distinguish price-depressing effects flowing from
inadequate internal outlets for investment from deflationary
pressures from the outside. Mere price deflation and unemployment is no proof of a disequilibrium in the exchange rate.

Consider now the case of a country that has a deficit in its
balance of payments. This condition is by no means proof that
its exchange rate is out of line. Its balance of payment position
may be due to a seriously depressed condition in some foreign
country that normally constitutes its best market. This could
be a cyclical matter and if so could probably reasonably well
be recognized as such. Or the deficit in its balance of payments
may be a chronic one owing to an unbalanced structure of
production. If this is the case, a change in the exchange rate is
not likely to be even temporarily, and especially in the long
run, of any significant value. What is needed is a realistic appraisal of the structure of the country's imports and exports.
Following such an analysis, it should be possible to find ways
and means of developing the natural resources of the country,
the required human skills, and the capital facilities necessary
to alter the structure of the imports and exports so as to promote
a balance in its international account. If the fundamental structure of a country's imports and exports is seriously out of balance, it would require perfectly enormous changes in the exchange rate in order to bring about equilibrium. Again, we are
back at the proposition that the price elasticity of exports and
imports may not be adequate to bring about equilibrium. Moreover, if a balance could be brought about by a change in the
exchange rate this might merely tend to perpetuate a serious
distortion of the structure of the economy of the country in

question. A thorough survey of the potential resources of the country, both human and material, the possibility of diversification of its agriculture and its industries in a broad developmental program, is certainly a more meaningful and realistic solution than to rely upon the weak reed of a change in the exchange rate.

The conclusion I reach, so far as the cycle is concerned, is that the introduction of exchange control to meet a temporary emergency may be preferred to the juggling of the foreign-exchange rate. And the solution of a chronic deficit in the balance of payments in many countries should be found in resource surveys and developmental programs. Beyond this, however, a country may, in fact, be suffering from a fundamental disequilibrium caused by an inappropriate exchange rate. And the real basis for determining whether such a disequilibrium exists is to be found in divergencies of the exchange rate from what I would call the cost-structure parity. The evidence of such disequilibrium would be an artificial price competitive pressure from abroad causing deflation and unemployment.

INDEX